Same Sex Marriage and Church Law:

A liberal evangelical call for greater inclusivity within Christianity according to scripture

Kevin Mahoney

Punked Books

Published in 2014 by Punked Books
An Authortrek imprint
www.authortrek.com/punked-books

Cover image ©istockphoto.com/Christophe Boisson

Third Edition

ISBN 978-1-908375-26-1

Scripture quotations are from the New Revised Standard Version Bible:
Anglicised Edition, copyright © 1989, 1995 the Division of Christian
Education of the National Council of the Churches of Christ in the United
States of America. Used by permission. All rights reserved.

For my Father,
who first inspired in me the power of justice

Justice will not be served until those who are unaffected
are as outraged as those who are.
Benjamin Franklin

Contents

Introduction

I have recently returned to the Christian faith after being away for nearly two decades, as I wanted to bring up my offspring as Christian. My parents raised me as a Catholic; however, I could not bring myself to return to Catholicism, as my outlook on life is far more liberal than that of the Holy See at this moment. It did not seem right to me to introduce any child of mine to a denomination that has no female priests, and one that is never likely to. My local church, St. George's in Chesterton, Cambridge, is Church of England, and this suited me fine, for I regard the Church of England as being far more liberal and inclusive than Catholicism. (Having written that, the Church of England's deliberations on promoting female clergy to the rank of bishop has been painfully slow, which I find remarkable, given that women are hardly a minority in society!)

Although I have had a longing to return to Christianity for ten years now, there has been one issue that has made me reluctant to return to the faith more than most, and that is Christianity's treatment of homosexuality. I am sure that I am not the only liberal Christian who has held back from professing their faith due to the fear that they would be seen as being suddenly intolerant of homosexuality by their gay friends and colleagues. I do not regard homosexuality as a sin; far from it. Indeed, I will be arguing in this book that the Christian Church should conduct and celebrate marriages between same sex couples. Obviously, there are several passages within the Bible that condemn homosexuality, which some conservative Christians have used to denounce same sex marriages. However, I will be discussing these passages at great length, in my bid to shed new light upon them, and to propose ways in which we can make this issue less divisive within Christianity.

Since I believe that the Christian church should place an emphasis on inclusivity, I argue that the church should celebrate "same sex marriage", instead of just "gay marriage". Although the Bible condemns homosexuality instead of say, bisexuality, transsexuality, or transgenderism, it would be remiss of me to leave out other sexual or gender orientations from my argument. For instance, a "same sex marriage" could be between two bisexuals, and so this term is more inclusive than "gay marriage". Although many gay people regard "homosexual" as a cold, clinical term, it was first used by the Austrian novelist Karl-Maria Kertbeny in a pamphlet in which he attacked a Prussian anti-gay law. Since I have written this book in the same anti-discriminatory spirit as Kertbeny, I feel that is apt to reclaim the word "homosexual", especially as some modern Bible editors have subverted this term by adopting it in Biblical passages that condemn gay people.

My main aim is to promote the loving inclusivity that is fundamental to Christianity, and to argue that this intolerance of homosexuality is an aberration and a huge impediment to a faith that is desperately in need of new young converts within the Western world.

Although I base my discussion of this issue within the context of Christianity within England, I believe and pray that my arguments will be of relevance to churches throughout the world that wrestle with the same dilemma. Also, since most of the laws against homosexuality around the world have a religious basis, then I believe that my defeat of the conservative Christian argument against homosexuality will be useful for non-religious gay rights campaigners too.

One: Homosexuality in the Bible

The Old Testament Condemnation of Homosexuality

If you are gay, then the Bible is very forbidding with regards to your sexuality. The first mention of homosexuality is in Leviticus 18:22:

> You shall not lie with a male as with a woman; it is an abomination. (NRSVA)

While on first appearances, this is a very clear condemnation of homosexuality, it is not without its problems. For instance, once you look at this passage a bit closer, then it becomes clearer that Moses meant this injunction for a male reader, as it does not make any sense if the reader is female. Scholars commonly ascribe the authorship of the first books of the Bible (the Pentateuch or Torah) to Moses. From Leviticus 18:22, it would seem clear that Moses did not address the Pentateuch to women, or if he did, then he regarded them as being very much in a minority in his readership. One can argue then, that 18:22 is indicative of Moses' discrimination against women, as well as homosexuals. Following their escape from slavery in Egypt, the Israelite culture was clearly patriarchal, especially when one considers that Moses had to give the daughters of Zelophehad special dispensation to inherit their father's property when he died without a male heir (although they were later restricted to only marrying men within their own clan, so that this property would not leave their tribe).

The Death Penalty as Punishment for Homosexuality

The next mention of homosexuality within Leviticus (20.13) is clearer, and grimmer in its pronouncement of the death penalty as punishment:

> If a man lies with a male as with a woman, both of them have committed an abomination; they shall be put to death; their blood is upon them. (NRSVA)

Indeed, this admonition is literally the 'killer statement', for it is difficult to get past it in this debate. According to Moses, the above statement is direct speech from the Lord, which he has faithfully transcribed. That one sentence above is the reason why many Christians with same sex attraction choose to remain celibate, and why the Church of England insists that gay clergy refrain from sexual activity.

Mosaic Laws that Christians do not follow: the Death Penalty for Rebellious Youth

Then again, the above injunction against homosexuality is not one of the Ten Commandments. Moses relayed many such laws that Christians (or anyone else, for that matter) do not obey. For instance, there is the example of Leviticus 20:9:

All who curse father or mother shall be put to death; having cursed father or mother, their blood is upon them. (NRSVA)

Now, if we were to follow such a law today, then the human race would undoubtedly soon become extinct, as very few people would be able to survive their teenage years! This is not a mistranslation or a slip of the pen, for Moses repeats this death sentence later in Deuteronomy (21:18-21):

If someone has a stubborn and rebellious son who will not obey his father and mother, who does not heed them when they discipline him, then his father and his mother shall take hold of him and bring him out to the elders of his town at the gate of that place. They shall say to the elders of his town, 'This son of ours is stubborn and rebellious. He will not obey us. He is a glutton and a drunkard.' Then all the men of the town shall stone him to death. So you shall purge the evil from your midst; and all Israel will hear, and be afraid. (NRSVA)

Moses' Struggles to Maintain Control over the Israelites

Moses wrote these laws at a time when he was struggling to keep control over the twelve tribes of Israel following their escape from Egypt. Moses, by his own admission, was not a great orator, who often relied on his older brother

Aaron to speak during his confrontations with the pharaoh. Even though Aaron was Moses' brother, he betrayed Moses by casting the statue of the Golden Calf that the Israelites worshipped during Moses' sojourn on Mount Sinai. In this way, Moses' leadership skills were so poor that he was not even able to command the loyalty of his own brother. Indeed, when the Lord first called upon Moses to lead the Israelites out of Egypt, Moses was fearful that they would not follow him, mainly due to his poor rhetoric (Exodus 4:10):

> But Moses said to the Lord, 'O my Lord, I have never been eloquent, neither in the past nor even now that you have spoken to your servant; but I am slow of speech and slow of tongue.' (NRSVA)

I have a great deal of empathy with Moses here in his confessions of his failings, as I am also a very poor public speaker. (You won't see me promoting my beliefs on Youtube as the more eloquent Biblical commentator Matthew Vines has recently done.)

Moses' Creation of a National Identity

Moses' purpose in laying down these laws was to create a national identity for the Israelites, according to his singular vision, which allowed no space for diversity of whatever kind. The twelve tribes of Israel wandered in the wilderness for forty years, and faced a constant battle for survival. Moses believed that keeping tight discipline was necessary for the twelve tribes to come through these harsh conditions when faced by enemies on all sides. It was an extreme situation that required extreme laws. These laws would seem to show that Moses needed the support of the older generation to keep the rebellious youth of Israel in check, or else he feared that the twelve tribes of Israel would disintegrate. Like many a politician today, Moses probably placed graver and graver admonitions on issues such as homosexuality to win the support and approval of those elders of Israel who regarded homosexuals, rebellious youths, and the like as sinners.

Flooding as Punishment from God

There are extremely conservative politicians who make similar pronouncements today. For instance, there is the example of the UKIP councillor (United Kingdom Independence Party) who blamed the floods that afflicted Southern England in 2014 on Prime Minister David Cameron for legalizing same sex marriage. It is no accident that this UKIP councillor chose to see flooding as God's punishment, for flooding is a very Biblical penalty. As Moses wrote in Genesis (6:5), God was so dismayed by the wickedness of humanity, that He sent the Great Flood to wash away every living thing on Earth. However, one man of virtue, Noah, and his family found favour with God, who instructed him to build the Ark to save his family and every living thing. When Noah's Ark found dry land, God made a new covenant with Noah (Genesis 9:11-16):

"I establish my covenant with you, that never again shall all flesh be cut off by the waters of a flood, and never again shall there be a flood to destroy the earth." God said, "This is the sign of the covenant that I make between me and you and every living creature that is with you, for all future generations: I have set my bow in the clouds, and it shall be a sign of the covenant between me and the earth. When I bring clouds over the earth and the bow is seen in the clouds, I will remember my covenant that is between me and you and every living creature of all flesh; and the waters shall never again become a flood to destroy all flesh. When the bow is in the clouds, I will see it and remember the everlasting covenant between God and every living creature of all flesh that is on the earth." (NRSVA)

Since God promised to never destroy the Earth again with a flood, I believe that any politicians who make such pronouncements about floods (or any other natural disasters) as punishment from God for homosexuality are very much misreading the Bible. Indeed, such extreme conservative commentators seem as if they are also mixing up the story of Noah's Ark with that of Sodom and Gomorrah (another infamous tale that I will discuss in more depth in Chapter Two).

The Covenant of the Rainbow and the Rainbow Flag

Incidentally, I think that it wonderful that the rainbow is not only the sign of God's covenant with humankind, but it is also a symbol that the Lesbian Gay

Bisexual Transgender community (LGBT) has adopted in the form of the Rainbow Flag. Admittedly, it seems as if there is no Biblical reference intended in the LGBT adoption of the rainbow, as the flag is more a symbol of diversity and Gay Pride. The rainbow flag's derivation has often been attributed to "Over the Rainbow", as sung by gay icon Judy Garland in *The Wizard of Oz*. And yet I think that there is possibly an unconscious Biblical aspect to the LGBT adoption of the rainbow as a symbol of hope.

The Lord Does Change His Mind

Although many liberal Christians regard Leviticus 20.13 as being highly discriminatory (at the very least), it is still difficult for us to argue with Moses's account of the Lord's words, for to do so is to call Moses a liar. In this way, it is possible to argue that since Moses had successfully led the Israelites to freedom from Egypt, he evidently had God's favour, which could have tempted Moses to use the Lord's name to pass such laws much more easily, especially since he could not rely on his poor public speaking skills to achieve his aims. Obviously, calling someone a liar is a far less serious offence than calling for the execution of gay people, but it is still uncomfortable for us to do with regards to the man who laid the foundation stones for the civilization in which Jesus lived. It may be that Moses just heard what he wanted to hear, according to the norms of the patriarchal culture of the Israelites. Then again, there is always the prospect that Moses transcribed the Lord's words faithfully, and that the Lord Himself issued this death sentence against homosexuality. Yet I must point out that it's quite clear from the Bible that humankind's relationship with the Lord has never been a static one. Indeed, we see from Moses's account of the Golden Calf incident that the Lord does change His mind about destroying His people when they plead for mercy, as Moses does here (Exodus 32:7-14):

The Lord said to Moses, 'Go down at once! Your people, whom you brought up out of the land of Egypt, have acted perversely; they have been quick to turn aside from the way that I commanded them; they have cast for themselves an image of a calf, and have worshipped it and sacrificed to it, and said, "These are your gods, O Israel, who brought you up out of the land of Egypt!"' The Lord said to Moses, 'I have seen this people, how stiff-necked they are. Now let me alone, so that my wrath may burn hot against them and I may consume them; and of you I will make a great nation.'

But Moses implored the Lord his God, and said, 'O Lord, why does your wrath burn hot against your people, whom you brought out of the land of Egypt with great power and with a mighty hand? Why should the Egyptians say, "It was with evil intent that he brought them out to kill them in the mountains, and to consume them from the face of the earth"? Turn from your fierce wrath; change your mind and do not bring disaster on your people. Remember Abraham, Isaac, and Israel, your servants, how you swore to them by your own self, saying to them, "I will multiply your descendants like the stars of heaven, and all this land that I have promised I will give to your descendants, and they shall inherit it for ever."' And the Lord changed his mind about the disaster that he planned to bring on his people. (NRSVA)

It may well be that homosexuality was not part of the Lord's original plan for humanity. Yet we see from the Bible that humankind interacted with the environment and with each other in many ways that the Lord had not anticipated. Anyone who has gay friends and colleagues will know that they have not adopted homosexuality as a 'lifestyle choice'; instead, their homosexuality seems inbuilt into them at a genetic level. Indeed, some scientists now believe that an evolutionary advantage to homosexuality is possible, which is why it is so prevalent within humanity and other species. Just as we evolve in ways that the Lord may not have anticipated, so it seems does our relationship with Him evolve likewise. Indeed, it is not surprising that our early relationship with God was very turbulent, for as Moses writes in Genesis 1:27, "So God created humankind in his image, in the image of God he created them; male and female he created them." It is not so much that we *look* like the Lord, but that we *act* like Him, especially when we achieved full sentience after we disobeyed Him by eating the fruit from the Tree of the Knowledge of Good and Evil. (Indeed, according to Moses' cosmogony in Genesis, the very reason why we are having this heated debate is because we ate from the Tree of the Knowledge of Good and Evil, which led to God expelling us from our carefree lifestyle in the idyllic Garden of Eden.

Certainly, because there are so many shades of grey in such issues of morality, we seem unable to universally agree what is good and evil about them, which leads to great stress and anger on both sides of such debates.) Obviously, although we act like the Lord, and are capable of surprising and angering Him, we will never be on an equal footing with our omnipotent Lord, and the only way that we can ever regain eternal life in paradise is by via our faith in Him, as Jesus taught us. Although the Lord did denounce homosexuality in Leviticus 20.13, I believe that He has listened to the pleadings of many throughout the centuries for mercy to gay people, just as He listened to Moses' pleas in Exodus 32:11-14. Certainly, as I will argue later, I see the hand of the Holy Spirit in the moves by legislators to abolish punitive laws against homosexuality and their recognition of same sex marriage. Certainly, there is no evil motive in the actions of these legislators; instead, I see a lot of Christian good within them. Then again, it may be that it was not the Lord, but ourselves that have always been against 'the Other' and differences such as homosexuality, and that until now, we have not been ready to listen and adhere to the plea for LGBT equality. Now that it is 2014, it seems that we are finally ready to move beyond Leviticus 20.13.

Paul's Reiteration of Moses' Laws

UKIP expelled the above councillor from the party in the wake of his comments about floods being God's punishment for the legalization of same sex marriage. At the time of writing this treatise, another severe critic of homosexuality, Westboro Baptist Church leader Fred Phelps, passed away. In its report on his death, the BBC stated that his "church... rose to international notoriety with its practice of picketing funerals of fallen US troops. It claimed their deaths were punishment for America's tolerance of gay people." Obviously, the Westboro Baptist Church took rather extreme methods in opposing toleration of homosexuality. However, more moderate conservative Christians, who regard the Bible as the literal Word of God, argue that these Biblical passages prove that God views homosexuality as sinful. One can counter this by arguing that the Old Testament relates God's previous covenants with humanity, and that Jesus gave us a new covenant that superseded them. Then again, St. Paul's first letter to the Romans is part of the New Testament, and when writing about 'The Guilt of Humankind', Paul very much repeated Moses' laws:

> For the wrath of God is revealed from heaven against all ungodliness and wickedness of those who by their wickedness suppress the truth. For what can be known about God is plain to them, because God has shown it to them. Ever since the creation of the world his eternal power and divine nature, invisible though they are, have been understood and seen through the things he has made. So they are without excuse; for though they knew God, they did not honour him as God or give thanks to him, but they became futile in their thinking, and their senseless minds were darkened. Claiming to be wise, they became fools; and they exchanged the glory of the immortal God for images resembling a mortal human being or birds or four-footed animals or reptiles.
>
> Therefore God gave them up in the lusts of their hearts to impurity, to the degrading of their bodies among themselves, because they exchanged the truth about God for a lie and worshiped and served the creature rather than the Creator, who is blessed forever! Amen.
>
> For this reason God gave them up to degrading passions. Their women exchanged natural intercourse for unnatural, and in the same way also the men, giving up natural intercourse with women, were consumed with passion for one another. Men committed shameless acts with men and received in their own persons the due penalty for their error.
>
> And since they did not see fit to acknowledge God, God gave them up to a debased mind and to things that should not be done. They were filled with every kind of wickedness, evil, covetousness, malice. Full of envy, murder, strife, deceit, craftiness, they are gossips, slanderers, God-haters, insolent, haughty, boastful, inventors of evil, rebellious toward parents, foolish, faithless, heartless, ruthless. They know God's decree, that those who practice such things deserve to die—yet they not only do them but even applaud others who practice them. (Romans 1:18-32, NRSVA)

Paul begins this passage by arguing that worshipping false idols leads humanity to all manners of sin. This is very much the same concern as Moses, who constantly had to admonish the Israelites for worshipping false idols (such as the Golden Calf) instead of God. As well as Moses' condemnation of homosexuality, there is again the rebuke of those "rebellious toward parents"; Paul repeats that those that rebel against their parents deserve to die according to God's decree as well as those that practice homosexuality. Although Paul begins Romans 1 by writing that Jesus called him to spread the Gospel, the end of the letter is in a very different tone from that of Jesus' teachings. Paul is reinforcing Moses' laws here (the admonition to cast aside false idols) because he is writing to the Roman church, since the Romans traditionally worshipped a multitude of gods. So, rather than telling the Roman church that they should condemn rebellious teenagers and homosexuals to death, he is instead vigorously reinforcing the point that they should only worship the one true God, and cast aside all other idols.

Paul's Condemnation of Homosexuality

Yet this is not the only passage in which Paul condemns homosexuality. In his letter to the Corinthians, Paul goes on to write:

> Do you not know that wrongdoers will not inherit the kingdom of God? Do not be deceived! Fornicators, idolaters, adulterers, male prostitutes, sodomites, thieves, the greedy, drunkards, revilers, robbers—none of these will inherit the kingdom of God. And this is what some of you used to be. But you were washed, you were sanctified, you were justified in the name of the Lord Jesus Christ and in the Spirit of our God. (1 Corinthians 6:9-11, NRSVA)

The first part of this letter consists of Paul rebuking members of the church of Corinth for issuing law suits against each other over issues such as fraud, and for taking these disputes to a civil secular court, for Paul feared that this would bring the young church into disrepute. The last part of the letter warns members of the church of Corinth against engaging in sexual promiscuity, and to basically advise them to have respect for their bodies. Note that in the above New Revised Standard translation, the editors have chosen to use the word 'sodomites' to refer to homosexuals, since the sin of Sodom has been commonly been interpreted as homosexuality (more on this in Chapter Two).

It is interesting to note here that scholars believe that Paul coined the Greek word arsenokoitēs (from the Greek for 'male', 'arsēn', and the Greek for 'bed', 'koitēs'). Since Paul was listing several 'sins', he probably devised this word as a shorthand way of referring to "a man [that] lies with a male as with a woman". (This seems to show that homosexuality really was not a big issue for the Israelites after all, if they had not invented a word for it before Paul.) You will also see that passage is a lot more positive than the first, as Paul does not say that homosexuals deserve to die here. Indeed, Paul informs the Corinthians that those of them that have sinned in the past have had their sins washed away by becoming Christians. Having written that, if like me, you believe that homosexuality is not a sin, then you will also believe that gay people have no need to repent for being gay. So, although Paul does say that gay people can inherit the kingdom of God, they can only do so by repenting their sexual identity. Indeed, this passage is often used by conservative Christians to call upon gay people to reject their homosexuality. This is clearly a form of repression. Conservative Christians tend to make this appeal for gay people to reject their sexuality in a well-mannered way, and with a sympathetic tone, but no matter how polite they are, these appeals are a torment, especially to young gay people as they begin to first acknowledge their inherent sexual identity.

Paul's Conflicting Messages on Homosexuality

One can argue here that Paul is quite contradictory in these two passages. In Romans 1, he says that homosexuals deserve to die, while in 1 Corinthians 6, Paul acknowledges that gay people will go to heaven, but only if they repent their homosexual identity. However, the reason for this change in tone is mainly because Paul is addressing two different audiences here. As I discussed above, Paul was very concerned that members of the Roman congregation would soon return to worshipping a multitude of gods, or would contrarily only add the one true God to their panoply of gods. So Paul's main concern when writing to the Romans was that this young Christian congregation would all too soon return to their Roman habits, and forget the one true God. In Corinthians, Paul still admonishes those that worship false idols (idolaters), but although there were statues and monuments of ancient Greek deities around this church, idolatry is not his main concern in a church that was not so directly influenced by the Roman way of life.

Just as Paul had an Epiphany, so can we

Paul's next mention of homosexuality is in his first letter to Timothy (1 Timothy 1:3-11):

> I urge you… to remain in Ephesus so that you may instruct certain people not to teach any different doctrine, and not to occupy themselves with myths and endless genealogies that promote speculations rather than the divine training that is known by faith. But the aim of such instruction is love that comes from a pure heart, a good conscience, and sincere faith. Some people have deviated from these and turned to meaningless talk, desiring to be teachers of the law, without understanding either what they are saying or the things about which they make assertions.

> Now we know that the law is good, if one uses it legitimately. This means understanding that the law is laid down not for the innocent but for the lawless and disobedient, for the godless and sinful, for the unholy and profane, for those who kill their father or mother, for murderers, fornicators, sodomites, slave-traders, liars, perjurers, and whatever else is contrary to the sound teaching that conforms to the glorious gospel of the blessed God, which he entrusted to me. (NRSVA)

Again, the translators of the New Revised Standard Version of the Bible have chosen to use the word "sodomites" to refer to homosexuals. I have no doubt that critics of my argument in this book will describe me as a "false teacher" who does not know what he is talking about. Yet I repeat that Paul is very unChristian in his condemnation of homosexuality, and that he is wrong to condemn gay people. St. Paul was not infallible; indeed, Paul had the most famous change of mind in history (his epiphany on the road to Damascus), when our Lord Jesus Christ called on him to spread the Gospel, instead of persecuting Christians as heretics. In this way, I argue that humankind should also have an epiphany, and that we should turn away from our historical homophobia. Paul displays a great deal of humility when he writes about his epiphany at the end of 1 Timothy 1(12-16):

I am grateful to Christ Jesus our Lord, who has strengthened me, because he judged me faithful and appointed me to his service, even though I was formerly a blasphemer, a persecutor, and a man of violence. But I received mercy because I had acted ignorantly in unbelief, and the grace of our Lord overflowed for me with the faith and love that are in Christ Jesus. The saying is sure and worthy of full acceptance, that Christ Jesus came into the world to save sinners—of whom I am the foremost. But for that very reason I received mercy, so that in me, as the foremost, Jesus Christ might display the utmost patience, making me an example to those who would come to believe in him for eternal life. (NRSV)

Paul was Still a Pharisee at Heart

When reading Paul's condemnation of homosexuality, it seems as though he has undertaken a kind of 'diplomatic revolution': although Paul has very much changed sides, by becoming Christianity's chief proponent instead of its chief prosecutor, it seems that his conservative nature (that led him to initially attack nascent Christianity) has not changed at all. As Paul wrote to the Philippians, before his conversion, he was "as to the law, a Pharisee" (Philippians 3:5). (I will be writing more about the Pharisees later in this book, as they form an integral part of my argument.) It is almost as if Paul uses the laws of Moses as a short-hand for all the ills of society, without conceding that there is a vast difference between a bloody murderer and say, a liar.

Paul's Views are not a New Christian Condemnation of Homosexuality

Indeed, from this perspective, Paul's views are not a new, Christian condemnation of homosexuality, for Paul is just repeating the old laws of Moses. Paul is also contrary to the teachings and examples of our Lord Jesus Christ, when he writes that "we know that the law is good, if one uses it legitimately. This means understanding that the law is laid down not for the *innocent* but for the lawless and disobedient, for the godless and sinful." When the Jewish elders of Jerusalem tried to catch Jesus out by presenting an adulteress before him (Moses proscribed that Israelites should punish adultery by stoning those found guilty to death), Jesus said that "Let anyone among

18

you who is without sin be the first to throw a stone at her." Since none of the adulteress' accusers could claim that they were without sin, they did not stone her. Jesus taught us that none of us, even the most pious and 'innocent' (to use Paul's term), are without sin. Although we are all sinners, the Lord will forgive us, as long as we repent of our sins. *At the end of the day, we are Christians, not Paulinians, and so where there is conflict between the teachings of Paul and our Lord, then we should give precedence to the words and actions of Jesus.*

Do Not Persecute Gay People

I call on conservative Christians that condemn homosexuality to pause for prayer and reflection; do not become "men of violence" (as Paul was before his epiphany), by stridently persecuting those in your community who are gay, for this is not the way of our Lord Jesus Christ. I especially urge those that call for the death penalty for homosexuality to think again, for our Lord opposed the use of capital punishment when presented with a case of sexual immorality, the adulteress. If your culture has traditionally demanded the death penalty for homosexuality, then I urge you to bravely follow Paul's example, to come to an epiphany, and turn your back on your culture, so that you save homosexuals from persecution, instead of condemning them.

Paul Retracts His Harsh Rhetoric

I am sure that Paul today would be horrified to learn that his letters (which he addressed to very specific audiences at the beginnings of the church) are still used today to persecute gay people. Paul's own letters express regret when the church at Corinth literally followed his below instructions to cast out sinners from among their flock (1 Corinthians 5:9-13):

I am writing to you not to associate with anyone who bears the name of brother or sister who is sexually immoral or greedy, or is an idolater, reviler, drunkard, or robber. Do not even eat with such a one. For what have I to do with judging those outside? Is it not those who are inside that you are to judge? God will judge those outside. 'Drive out the wicked person from among you.' (NRSVA)

This case involved a Christian who was sleeping with his father's wife. It very much appears that Paul is recalling and quoting Moses' punishment for sexual immorality here, from Leviticus 18:29 – "For whoever commits any of these abominations shall be cut off from their people" (NRSVA). Thankfully, the church at Corinth did not follow Paul's earlier exhortation to "hand this man over to Satan for the destruction of the flesh, so that his spirit may be saved on the day of the Lord" (1 Corinthians 5:5). However, the Corinthians did expel this incestuous man from their church, which caused Paul to later retract his earlier harsh condemnation of this sinner (2 Corinthians 2: 6-10):

> This punishment by the majority is enough for such a person; so now instead you should forgive and console him, so that he may not be overwhelmed by excessive sorrow. So I urge you to reaffirm your love for him. I wrote for this reason: to test you and to know whether you are obedient in everything. Anyone whom you forgive, I also forgive. (NRSV)

Paul appears as if he is excessively conservative here at first, by calling for churches to expel the sexually immoral from their congregations. Yet Paul later tells the young church that they should forgive those of their congregation that have repented of their sexual immorality. Although Paul earlier called upon the Corinthians to expel this incestuous man according to the laws of Moses, Paul later expressed the loving redemption offered by our Lord Jesus Christ. By forgiving this unfortunate young man, Paul revised the laws of Moses. So I call on conservative Christian leaders not to exile gay people from your church or community, but to engage with them in the light of our Lord Jesus Christ.

Paul Brought to Book by Corinth

Having written that, there is a possibility that the Corinthians replied to Paul, complaining that they thought his punishment for the incestuous member of their flock was excessive, and that they had already forgiven him following his repentance. Indeed, the Corinthians may have pleaded for Paul to allow this incestuous man to return to their flock, and for Paul to forgive this sinner, according to the teachings of Jesus. Paul's defence that he was just wanted to "test" the Corinthians is typical of someone in authority caught out advising an incorrect course of action. In this way, Paul's second epistle to the Corinthians has a modern tone; it is very possible that human behaviour in situations like this has been very consistent over the last two thousand years! It is also likely that Paul was afraid that a sex scandal could lead outside forces to destroy this fragile young church, in the same way that Paul worried that the early Christians would bring themselves into disrepute by bringing legal cases against each other in civil courts. In other words, Paul was too harsh here, due to him being understandably overprotective of the early Church. (Moses' harshness could also be due to him being overprotective towards the delicate society of the early Israelites.)

Paul's Theology not Written in Stone

Prior to Paul urging the church at Corinth not to associate with any of their flock who was immoral, he stated that "I wrote to you in my letter not to associate with sexually immoral persons— not at all meaning the immoral of this world, or the greedy and robbers, or idolaters, since you would then need to go out of the world" (1 Corinthians 5:9-10, NRSVA). So, Paul's theology was not written in stone: he changed it when a congregation took what he had written too 'literally'. Contrary to Jesus, who recognised that we are all sinners, Paul appears to assume that once someone has joined the church (after repenting their sins), then they would be not inclined to sin again. While this inclination is true of all churchgoers, and does reduce how much we sin, we still do sin, no matter how pious we are, such as those Jewish elders who tried to catch Jesus out by presenting him with an adulterous woman. Yet I must point out that Jesus did ask the adulterous woman to repent of her sin, and this will prompt some conservative Christians to say that they will not accept gay people until they have repented of their sin of 'homosexuality'. For instance, the Church of England accepts gay clergy, but only if they remain celibate. However homosexuality, unlike adultery, is not sinful, since it does not involve lies and deceit.

The False Pride of the Pharisees

Paul's advice not to 'mix with the wrong crowd' is also contrary to the actions

21

of our Lord Jesus Christ, who commonly associated with sinners and those traditionally regarded as 'unclean' by the Jewish community. My example of this is in Mark 2:15-17:

> And as he sat at dinner in Levi's house, many tax-collectors and sinners were also sitting with Jesus and his disciples—for there were many who followed him. When the scribes of the Pharisees saw that he was eating with sinners and tax-collectors, they said to his disciples, 'Why does he eat with tax-collectors and sinners?' When Jesus heard this, he said to them, 'Those who are well have no need of a physician, but those who are sick; I have come to call not the righteous but sinners. (NRSVA)

So, Jesus made a point of offering salvation to sinners, and socialized with them so that he could convert and save them. (Tax collectors were Jews who collected money for the Roman authorities, and so the Jews despised them, as they saw them as collaborators.) Jesus' actions seem to subvert what Paul later writes about avoiding the wrong crowd, for it was only by socializing with sinners that Jesus was able to convert them, so modern Christians should offer an open and inclusive door to everyone in the same way. Some conservative Christians might argue that to do so may leave them liable to corruption by sinners, for none of us are as resistant to temptation as our Lord Jesus Christ; but I believe that this corruption will only happen if your faith is weak. Conservative Christians might argue that the above passage only reinforces Paul's point that righteous, pious people, do not need to fear Moses' laws. However, I must reiterate that no one is without sin, including the Jewish elders (the Pharisees) who sought to catch Jesus out by presenting him with the adulterous woman. I can reinforce this argument with another of Jesus' teachings, the Parable of the Pharisee and the Tax Collector (Luke 18:9-14):

> He also told this parable to some who trusted in themselves that they were righteous and regarded others with contempt: 'Two men went up to the temple to pray, one a Pharisee and the other a tax-collector. The Pharisee, standing by himself, was praying thus, "God, I thank you that I am not like other people: thieves, rogues, adulterers, or even like this tax-collector. I fast twice a week; I give a tenth of all my income." But the tax-collector, standing far off, would not even look up to heaven, but was beating his

breast and saying, "God, be merciful to me, a sinner!" I tell you, this man went down to his home justified rather than the other; for all who exalt themselves will be humbled, but all who humble themselves will be exalted. (NRSVA)

In this way, I call on conservative Christians not to look down upon gay people with disgust, for as in the above example, this false pride is a sin.

Moses' Condemnation of Homosexuality not Universal

There is evidence in the Bible that Moses' law on homosexuality was only meant to apply to the Israelites themselves:

None of the daughters of Israel shall be a temple prostitute; none of the sons of Israel shall be a temple prostitute. You shall not bring the fee of a prostitute or the wages of a male prostitute into the house of the Lord your God in payment for any vow, for both of these are abhorrent to the Lord your God. (Deuteronomy 23:17-18, NRSV)

Although there is an injunction here against Israelites becoming temple prostitutes, there is no instruction to stone these temple prostitutes to death, whether they were male or female. So this indicates that Moses only intended that the Israelites should take heed of this law. Since Moses' law against homosexuality was not universal, it did not apply to foreigners. However, there is also the implication that Israelites visited these temple prostitutes, but there is no mention of stoning these prostitutes' clients; perhaps it is not so surprising that 'double standards' were practiced in such a patriarchal society. This form of temple prostitution was a foreign practice that those within the Jewish temple surprisingly adopted from time to time. (On a side note, some commentators think that the centurion's servant whose life Jesus saved may have been the Roman's homosexual lover, while others believe that relationship between David and Jonathan in the Book of Samuel could be a homosexual one. However, if these relationships were homosexual, then this is not made explicit in the text, especially in the case of David and Jonathan, probably because of Moses' prohibition of homosexuality.)

Moses' Condemnation of Transvestism in a New Light

Moses did not only condemn homosexuality, but also transvestism (Deuteronomy 22:5, NRSVA): "A woman shall not wear a man's apparel, nor shall a man put on a woman's garment; for whoever does such things is abhorrent to the Lord your God." Although this injunction against transvestism is quite dispiriting, one could argue that it is also quite reassuring, since writers have written about transvestism, like homosexuality, throughout human history. So neither homosexuality nor transvestism can be taken to be a sign of a decadent modern culture (as some conservative Christians accuse the West of being), as homosexuality and transvestism occur in all cultures.

The West is Casting Aside its Previous Homophobia

Thankfully, we in the West tend are now more liberal and open about LGBT issues; however, it was not so long ago that we in the West persecuted homosexuality. For instance, the British forefather of modern computing, Alan Turing (who played a huge role in the code breaking efforts against the Nazis during the Second World War) chose chemical castration instead of imprisonment after he was found guilty of homosexuality in 1952. Such was his anguish at this treatment that Turing committed suicide in 1954. However, in 2013, Turing was finally granted a posthumous royal pardon, which is a great sign of how much has changed within British culture during the last sixty years.

Within my lifetime, the British Conservative party introduced Section 28, a law which stated that local authorities "shall not intentionally promote homosexuality or publish material with the intention of promoting homosexuality". Incredibly, this 1988 law was only repealed in the UK in 2003. In 2013, Russia introduced legislation that was very similar in tone to Section 28, which banned the "propaganda of non-traditional sexual relations" among children. This law effectively means that any demonstration for LGBT rights is illegal in Russia. However, there is some hope that Russia will repeal this law, if Section 28 is anything to go by. For instance, although David Cameron was against the repeal of Section 28 in 2003, by 2009, the prime minister-in-waiting had very much changed his mind, saying "we may have made mistakes, including Section 28". In 2013, David Cameron went on to introduce legislation that legalized civil same sex marriage services in the UK.

The Church of England's Discriminatory Laws Compared with Moses'

In the light of these fundamental changes in British society, the Church of England's ruling that gay clergy remain celibate (which is not applied to heterosexual clergy) looks very discriminatory. The Labour MP Ben Bradshaw is also challenging the Church of England's policy on same sex marriages, asking if they really would defrock a vicar who married a same sex partner. The Church of England would never discriminate against a priest with disabilities, as this would be indefensible. However, one of Moses' rulings in Leviticus (21:17-23) proscribed disabled people from becoming priests:

No one of your offspring throughout their generations who has a blemish may approach to offer the food of his God. For no one who has a blemish shall draw near, one who is blind or lame, or one who has a mutilated face or a limb too long, or one who has a broken foot or a broken hand, or a hunchback, or a dwarf, or a man with a blemish in his eyes or an itching disease or scabs or crushed testicles. No descendant of Aaron the priest who has a blemish shall come near to offer the Lord's offerings by fire; since he has a blemish, he shall not come near to offer the food of his God. He may eat the food of his God, of the most holy as well as of the holy. But he shall not come near the curtain or approach the altar, because he has a blemish, that he may not profane my sanctuaries; for I am the Lord; I sanctify them. (NRSVA)

Moses disseminated the above ruling for the Israelites in the wilderness, so it was not meant to become universal or everlasting. No one would use this passage today to defend the banning of a person with disabilities from becoming a vicar or a rabbi, which is a great sign of how our sensibilities have changed since Biblical times, mainly through the love and understanding of our Lord Jesus Christ. So, I say to conservative Christians, think about how hurtful the above passage is for disabled people, for gay people feel the same hurt when they read Biblical passages condemning homosexuality.

The Church of England Ignores Paul's Injunctions against Women

As well as this prohibition against disabled priests, there are other aspects of the Bible today that reforming churches disregard. For instance, the Church of England today ignores Paul's injunction that Christians should not allow women to speak in church:

> As in all the churches of the saints, women should be silent in the churches. For they are not permitted to speak, but should be subordinate, as the law also says. If there is anything they desire to know, let them ask their husbands at home. For it is shameful for a woman to speak in church. (1 Corinthians 14:33-35, NRSVA)

> I permit no woman to teach or to have authority over a man; she is to keep silent. For Adam was formed first, then Eve; and Adam was not deceived, but the woman was deceived and became a transgressor. Yet she will be saved through childbearing, provided they continue in faith and love and holiness, with modesty. (1 Timothy 2:12-15, NRSVA)

It is twenty years now since the Church of England first ordained women priests, contrary to Paul's rather sexist views in the above epistles. Indeed, many conservative Christian clergy have used Paul's views to support their refusal to serve under a woman bishop. It appears that under the current proposals for women bishops, such conservative male clergy may face disciplinary action if they refuse to serve under a woman bishop, such is the Church of England's urgency to pass this motion after the House of Laity controversially voted against it in 2012. However, as late as 2011 the Archbishop of Canterbury Rowan Williams appointed two new "flying bishops" (Provincial Episcopal Visitors that offer pastoral care to clergy, laity and parishes that do not accept women priests), after two previous incumbents of this role joined the Roman Catholic church. (Where will these two jump ship if the Roman Catholic Church starts ordaining women?) Having written that, it is refreshing to read in a report from *The Guardian* newspaper in 2011 that only 2.8% of parishes had requested the services of a flying bishop. I hope and pray that the Church of England will abolish such an office that openly discriminates against women in the years to come, and that they will finally appoint women bishops. Just as the Synod of the Church of England has ignored Paul's injunctions about silencing women in church, so I hope and pray that they will also ignore Moses' laws against homosexuality, and to allow same sex marriages in church. Yet, as I have written before, if it has taken the Church of England over twenty years to promote women (who are hardly a minority in society) to the office of bishop, then how long will it take for them to let go of Moses' unjust condemnation of homosexuality?

Paul's Declaration of Equality is Still Binding

It would be wrong to decry Paul as nothing but a conservative killjoy, for, while spreading the Gospel, he did write some very illuminating and liberating passages, such as Galatians 3:2 – "There is no longer Jew or Greek, there is no longer slave or free, there is no longer male and female; for all of you are one in Christ Jesus" (NRSVA). Campaigners for female clergy used Paul's declaration of equality in support of their argument. The British MP William Wilberforce certainly found Galatians 3:2 useful in his bid to abolish the slave trade, along with Paul's first epistle to Timothy, where Paul condemned slave traders. (As mentioned before, Paul also condemned 'sodomites', i.e., homosexuals, immediately before his denunciation of slave traders.) However, Paul did not censure slavery outright, which those on the other side in the slavery debate used to defend their sinful trade. As I have mentioned before, it is not surprising that Paul contradicted himself when writing about, say the role of women, as he wrote many letters, which he intended for different audiences. Paul did not intend his words of guidance to a young church to still be taken literally two thousand years later. Indeed, Paul may have thought such worship of his words as idolatrous.

Moses' Mercy for Escaped Slaves Integral to Defeat of Slavery

Slave owners found other passages in the Bible very useful for defending their despicable trade, including the revelation that the Israelites, despite their bondage in Egypt, maintained their custom of owning slaves after Moses had led them to freedom. However, there is also a passage in Moses' laws that revealed that he had a more liberal approach to slaves than other forms of property, such as cattle (according to Deuteronomy 22, people who found cattle that had strayed from their fields, were to keep them safe until their owners claimed them), which is perhaps derived from the Israelites' own escape from bondage in Egypt (Deuteronomy 23, 15-16):

Slaves who have escaped to you from their owners shall not be given back to them. They shall reside with you, in your midst, in any place they choose in any one of your towns, wherever they please; you shall not oppress them. (NRSVA)

Although Moses' injunction to treat escaped slaves with dignity and respect appears to fly in the face of his other, more patriarchal orders, I was not surprised to read the above passage, as I had expected to come across a more liberal attitude to slavery from Moses than other issues. Do not forget that Moses was so fired up by the Egyptians' despicable treatment of their Hebrew slaves that he actually murdered an Egyptian who had assaulted an Israelite. The same fire burned in his belly when God called on Moses to lead the Israelites' exodus from Egypt. Since he was so emotionally invested in the issue of Israelite slavery, it is not surprising to discover that Moses had a more liberal attitude to escaped slaves than he did to homosexuals, about whom he evidently knew very little. If perhaps a member of Moses' family had been openly gay, then he may have had a more understanding attitude to homosexuality. Unfortunately, this was not the case, and it is this lack of understanding that led him (and many others before and since) to denounce homosexuality. No doubt the above passage was a huge inspiration to those who took part in the Underground Railroad that helped the escape of many slaves from servitude in the United States during the 19th Century. Slavery was the norm in the both the Old Testament and New Testament eras (especially since slavery was very much part of Roman culture), but thankfully this sinful behaviour has been mostly eradicated. Indeed, I think this is what Moses hoped when he wrote (Deuteronomy 24, 7):

If someone is caught kidnapping another Israelite, enslaving or selling the Israelite, then that kidnapper shall die. So you shall purge the evil from your midst. (NRSVA)

Although slave traders no doubt took the above injunction to mean that it is permissible to enslave foreigners.

We Should Consign Homophobia, like Slavery, to History

It is very painful that slave owners and traders ever misused the Bible to spread the despicable practice of slavery, which caused the suffering of millions. Although it was customary to own slaves in Biblical times, I pray that nations will never return to this invidious practice. Just as we now see how evil slavery is, I hope and pray that one day we will see a world where homosexuals are no longer persecuted, and that like slavery, homophobia will be one Biblical custom that is mostly consigned to history.

Moses' Laws and Masculinity

As I mentioned before with regards to the stoning of rebellious teenagers, there are many of Moses' laws that even the most conservative Christian or Jew would never apply. For instance, there is Deuteronomy 25:11-12, which states:

> If men get into a fight with one another, and the wife of one intervenes to rescue her husband from the grip of his opponent by reaching out and seizing his genitals, you shall cut off her hand; show no pity. (NRSVA)

This is a very severe punishment for what most of us would regard as an act of self-defence. Perhaps the punishment is so strict because this hypothetical woman touches the sexual organ of a man other than her husband. Indeed, Moses must have meant this as a sexual prohibition, as there is no mention of a similar sanction for a man committing the same action. Then again, Moses could be presuming here that a man would never do such a thing to another man. I am not referring here to the momentary, startling pain that a man feels when his testicles are hit with force. Instead, I am talking about a running theme in Moses' laws, which states that men with permanently crushed testicles cannot become priests (as discussed earlier with regards to Leviticus 21:17-23), which Moses repeated in Deuteronomy 23:1 – "No one whose testicles are crushed or whose penis is cut off shall be admitted to the assembly of the Lord". In the very patriarchal, masculine society of the early

Israelites, it would seem that such a man with a literal impotence would not allowed to hold an office of civil or priestly power, so making him doubly impotent in this way. This could be why Moses called also for the Israelites to exile homosexuals (among others that he considered as sexually deviant) in Leviticus and sentenced to death in Deuteronomy, possibly because he did not consider them 'manly' enough, or maybe because such men would be unlikely to raise children, and thus would be unable to add to the growth of the Israelite community, or pass on property to their heirs. This theme of rampant masculinity continues in Moses' final blessing for the tribe of Levi, where Moses calls for the *crushing* of adversaries' *loins*, "so that they do not rise again" (Deuteronomy 33:11):

> Bless, O Lord, his substance,
> and accept the work of his hands;
> crush the loins of his adversaries,
> of those that hate him, so that they do not rise again. (NRSVA)

Moses explicitly made priestly power hereditary among the tribe of Levi, so this could explain why Moses repeats the injunction against impotent men becoming priests, for such priests would not raise any sons to succeed them. Although these Israelite priests were very different in their functions from modern Christian clergy (since they mostly butchered and sacrificed animals to atone for Israelite sins, which Moses poetically refers to in his above blessing for the tribe of Levi), I must note that the Roman Catholic Church took a contrary view to the law of Moses by demanding that its clergy be celibate, mainly due to Christ's mention of eunuchs (Matthew 19:12):

> For there are eunuchs who have been so from birth, and there are eunuchs who have been made eunuchs by others, and there are eunuchs who have made themselves eunuchs for the sake of the kingdom of heaven. Let anyone accept this who can. (NRSVA)

Jesus Made Marriage More Just for Women

Some commentators believe that Jesus was referring to gay people when he said that "there are eunuchs who have been so from birth". However, if our

Lord Jesus Christ was referring to gay people here, then He was not very explicit. In any case, the above passage, where Jesus explains why some people never marry, is obviously not a good example to use in a book like this, whose main argument is that religious authorities should allow same sex marriages in church. Having written that, the context of the above passage involved the Jewish elders testing Jesus to see if he would reiterate Moses' divorce law. Importantly for my viewpoint in this book, Jesus does then go on to critique Moses' divorce law for being unjust. However, instead of making Moses' divorce law more liberal, Jesus pronounces that Moses made it too easy for an Israelite to divorce his wife, and says that a man should only divorce his wife in the case of marital infidelity. Jesus' disciples then comically complain (in a typical masculine way) that such conditions would make marriage impossible! What is unspoken here is that by making it more difficult for men to divorce, Jesus was protecting the women who would otherwise have been cast off by their husbands. In this way, Jesus was making marriage more just for wives in an era when women had few rights, such as the power to divorce abusive husbands. So, although Jesus did uphold the laws of Moses, he did critique them for being unjust, just as he prevented the stoning of the adulterous woman by asking those of her accusers without sin to throw the first stone. Jesus talks of marriage between a man and a woman, because, obviously enough, there was no same sex marriage in Jesus' day. (His disciples were very shocked by the expectation that they would have to remain married to the same woman for the rest of their lives. In this light, it is not surprising that Jesus did not say anything about same sex marriage, because his disciples did not live in a culture that could comprehend the need for such a union. Indeed, it has taken humankind an additional two thousand years to embrace this concept.) However, I argue that if two people of the same sex consent to marry one another, then they are making the same commitment that a heterosexual couple does. If two same sex partners feel that they have been called by God to marry in a church, then I feel I must reiterate what Jesus said: "Therefore what God has joined together, let no one separate" (Mark 10:9).

Gay People No Longer Outcast as Part of Jesus's New Covenant

The prophet Isaiah later revised Moses' exclusion of impotent men from the

Israelite Assembly, in the light of the coming Messiah (Isaiah 56:5-6):

> To the eunuchs who keep my sabbaths,
> who choose the things that please me
> and hold fast my covenant,
> I will give, in my house and within my walls,
> a monument and a name
> better than sons and daughters;
> I will give them an everlasting name
> that shall not be cut off. (NRSVA)

Note how cleverly and poetically that Isaiah refers to the act of castration. In addition to this, Moses pronounced that illegitimate offspring should also be expelled from the Assembly of the Lord, just like eunuchs (Deuteronomy 23:2):

> Those born of an illicit union shall not be admitted to the assembly of the Lord. Even to the tenth generation, none of their descendants shall be admitted to the assembly of the Lord. (NRSVA)

This is a harsh edict to prevent illegitimate children attending the assemblies of the Israelites, and is one which I am sure the Israelites never fully implemented, for it would be very difficult to police. Still, I am sure that priests in the Middle Ages would have used the above passage to force couples into matrimony, for fear that their children would be forever excluded from church. Like the law of Moses to expel homosexuals, the above order to exclude the offspring of illicit unions from the Israelite assembly is very unfair. It is certainly not a direction that even the most conservative Christian leader would follow today, especially not as this order was also revised by the prophet Isaiah:

> all who keep the sabbath, and do not profane it,
> and hold fast my covenant—
> these I will bring to my holy mountain,
> and make them joyful in my house of prayer;
> their burnt-offerings and their sacrifices

will be accepted on my altar;
for my house shall be called a house of prayer
for all peoples.
Thus says the Lord God,
who gathers the outcasts of Israel,
I will gather others to them
besides those already gathered.
(Isaiah 56:6-8, NRSVA).

Indeed, Isaiah 56 begins in the follow way (1-2):

Thus says the Lord:
Maintain justice, and do what is right,
for soon my salvation will come,
and my deliverance be revealed.

Happy is the mortal who does this,
the one who holds it fast,
who keeps the sabbath, not profaning it,
and refrains from doing any evil.

So I say to conservative Christian leaders not to cast out gay people from your community, but to treat them justly and hospitably, just as our Lord Jesus Christ (whose coming was foretold by Isaiah) would have done.

Christians Have Already Abandoned Much of Moses Despite the Opposition of the Pharisees

In addition to this, Christianity has previously abandoned various laws and ordinances of Moses that they believed that gentiles (non-Jews) would not accept upon embracing the faith. The most notable example is that gentiles no longer faced the Abrahamic\Israelite ritual of male circumcision that Moses reinforced, since this is an operation that could very well prove fatal at a time when conditions were less sanitary, with no access to antiseptic or antibiotics. The Apostles made their decision to abandon the ritual of circumcision for gentile converts to Christianity at the Council of Jerusalem in 50 AD:

33

Then certain individuals came down from Judea and were teaching the brothers, 'Unless you are circumcised according to the custom of Moses, you cannot be saved.' And after Paul and Barnabas had no small dissension and debate with them, Paul and Barnabas and some of the others were appointed to go up to Jerusalem to discuss this question with the apostles and the elders... When they came to Jerusalem, they were welcomed by the church and the apostles and the elders, and they reported all that God had done with them. But some believers who belonged to the sect of the Pharisees stood up and said, 'It is necessary for them to be circumcised and ordered to keep the law of Moses.'

The apostles and the elders met together to consider this matter. After there had been much debate, Peter stood up and said to them, 'My brothers, you know that in the early days God made a choice among you, that I should be the one through whom the Gentiles would hear the message of the good news and become believers. And God, who knows the human heart, testified to them by giving them the Holy Spirit, just as he did to us; and in cleansing their hearts by faith he has made no distinction between them and us. Now therefore why are you putting God to the test by placing on the neck of the disciples a yoke that neither our ancestors nor we have been able to bear? On the contrary, we believe that we will be saved through the grace of the Lord Jesus, just as they will.' (Acts 15:1-11, NRSVA)

Below is the pronouncement made by Jesus' apostle, James the Just (who some scholars believe was James, the brother of Jesus):

"Therefore my judgment is that we don't trouble those from among the Gentiles who turn to God, but that we write to them that they abstain from the pollution of idols, from sexual immorality, from what is strangled, and from blood. For Moses from generations of old has in every city those who preach him, being read in the synagogues every Sabbath." (Acts 15:19-21, WEB)

*

The Prohibition against Sexual Immorality

So, Jesus' Apostles no longer required gentiles to follow the law of Moses, except for those against idolatry, a couple of the dietary requirements, and (and importantly for my argument in this book) sexual immorality. This is why conservative Christians, such as Paul, still frowned on homosexuality. (I chose the WEB edition of the Bible here because it uses the more regular translation of "sexual immorality" instead of the NRSVA's "fornication".) However, I must note that Paul was one of the main proponents against gentiles having to follow Moses' laws, as he found them a great obstacle to his conversion of gentiles. Although James proposed that gentiles had no need to follow the law of Moses for salvation, he stated that he had no doubt the law of Moses would never die out, for Jewish religious leaders would still teach Moses from the synagogues. James was correct, since the law of Moses is still part of the Christian Bible. However, the law of Moses only really remains in the Bible today so that Christians can fully understand the culture and context of the society that Jesus lived in.

The Law of Moses No Longer Applies to Christians

The law of Moses, as James the Just ruled, does not apply to Christians today, especially since, as St. Peter pointed out, even the Israelites were never able to withstand the *unbearable yoke* of Moses' laws. Jesus's own apostles rejected the law of Moses at the Council of Jerusalem, as they believed Christ's Gospel amended the Lord's previous injunctions to humankind, except for the Ten Commandments. Although James the Just's ruling is that gentiles should still be warned against "sexual immorality", it seems as though he is telling the apostles that it is not necessary to use Moses' own definition of sexual immorality. So, I believe this means that modern church councils are free to decide for themselves what they mean by "sexual immortality".

Modern Churches' Discrimination against Same Sex Couples Condemned in Scripture

Do not forget that the most common definition of "fornication" is sexual intercourse outside of marriage between consenting adults. If modern churches do not allow same sex couples to marry in church, then this means that Christian same sex couples will have to forever deny their natural urges, despite most modern churches no longer even forbidding premarital sex between heterosexual couples. This is another way in which modern churches discriminate against same sex couples, which is contrary to the writings of James the Just (The Letter of James, 2:8-9):

You do well if you really fulfil the royal law according to the scripture, 'You shall love your neighbour as yourself.' But if you show partiality, you commit sin and are convicted by the law as transgressors. (NRSVA)

Although James was warning about giving preferential treatment to wealthy people in the above instance, it follows that the church should also be impartial to people's sexual orientation, and so should not act more favourably to heterosexuals by allowing them marital bliss, while denying this to same sex couples.

A New Definition of 'Sexual Immorality'

Some Biblical commentators say that James' Apostolic Decree meant that gentiles now only had to follow the Seven Laws of Noah, which predate Moses' laws. The laws that God laid down for Noah and his descendants (i.e., everyone) were that they were forbidden from cursing God, worshipping false idols (i.e., other gods), murder, theft, eating the flesh of a live animal, and (importantly here) sexual immorality. God also ordered that humankind should create law courts to settle disputes. Since these Noahide Laws predate the laws of Moses, I argue again that this means that Moses' condemnation of homosexuality does not apply to modern Christians. As Moses' condemnation of homosexuality is a barrier to converting people in the West to Christianity, I hereby argue that the church should abandon Moses' condemnation of homosexuality (and its reiteration by Paul), under the precedent set down by the Apostolic Council of 50 AD. These Noahide Laws are the covenant (promise) that God signified with the symbol of the Rainbow. In the light of this conjunction with the LGBT adoption of the Rainbow symbol, I propose that our definition of "sexual immorality" be updated, as our understanding of sexual immorality has changed a great deal in the three

36

thousand years since Moses. I will discuss this new definition of "sexual immorality" in the next chapter.

Two: Sodom - Liberal Christianity is not a Sexual Free-for-All – the prohibition against paedophilia, rape, incest, and adultery

The Historic Equation of Sodomy with Homosexuality

As I mentioned in the Introduction, the Austrian novelist Karl-Maria Kertbeny first used the term "homosexual" in a pamphlet in which he condemned Prussian anti-Sodomy laws. Prior to Kertbeny, conservative Christians often used the term "sodomite" to mean "homosexual". The reason for this is that these conservative Christians thought that the main sin of the Sodomites, which led to God to destroy their city out of punishment for their wickedness, was homosexuality. You can see why they thought this when you read this extract from the Bible, which tells of Sodom's destruction (Genesis 19:1-11):

> The two angels came to Sodom in the evening, and Lot was sitting in the gateway of Sodom. When Lot saw them, he rose to meet them, and bowed down with his face to the ground. He said, 'Please, my lords, turn aside to your servant's house and spend the night, and wash your feet; then you can rise early and go on your way.' They said, 'No; we will spend the night in the square.' But he urged them strongly; so they turned aside to him and entered his house... But before they lay down, the men of the city, the men of Sodom, both young and old, all the people to the last man, surrounded the house; and they called to Lot, 'Where are the men who came to you tonight? Bring them out to us, so that we may know them.' Lot went out of the door to the men, shut the door after him, and said, 'I beg you, my brothers, do not act so wickedly. Look, I have two daughters who have not known a man; let me bring them out to you, and do to them as you please; only do nothing to these men, for they have come under the shelter of my roof.' But they replied, 'Stand back!' And they said, 'This fellow came here as an alien, and he would play the judge! Now we will deal worse with you than with them.' Then they pressed hard against the man Lot, and came near the door to break it down. But the men inside reached out their hands and brought Lot into the house with them, and shut the door. And they struck with blindness the men who were at the door of the house, both small and great, so that they were unable to find the door. (NRSVA)

Bible translators agree that when the men of Sodom call to Lot to bring out the angels "so that we may know them," this means that the Sodomites wanted to rape the two angels. To save his guests, Lot ingloriously offers his two daughters to the crowd, so that they would molest them instead of the angels. (One would have thought that it would have been far more self-sacrificial if Lot had offered himself up for molestation by the crowd, rather than cowardly offering up his daughters.) It is the Sodomite crowd's refusal of this wretched offer to molest Lot's daughters that has led many conservative commentators to believe that the Sodomites were intent on homosexual rape. Although scholars believe that angelic messengers from God are genderless and without material substance, these two angels manifested themselves in masculine form while visiting Sodom for some unknown reason. Certainly the crowd of Sodomite men see Lot's two visitors as having a masculine appearance, and this too reinforces the idea that the Sodomites were intent on homosexual rape.

The Depiction of Angels in Art

(One could write a whole book about how Western artists have depicted angels. Artists throughout history have represented angels as men, and wearing martial gear such as breastplates; however, Biblical scholars write that angels are genderless and without material substance. To complicate matters, parents have used the names of angels such as Michael, Gabriel, and Raphael, for male children. Yet artists often depict angels in art as having long, flowing hair; so much so that these pictures of angels that artists meant to portray as masculine figures, look transsexual to us now. There is also the commonplace depiction of angels as women in the form of Victorian graveyard statues, which was probably derived from Coventry Patmore's archetypal 1854 work *The Angel of the House*. This poem depicted a model of wifely feminine domesticity and submission to her husband that was very popular in an era that was very patriarchal, despite having a woman as head of state in the UK. Artists depicted angels with wings as a reference to the attributes of the Greek god Hermes and the Roman god Mercury, because Hermes, like an angel, was a heavenly messenger, and this was how they supposed he flew from the heavens to Earth. Moses said that God did not want humankind to make images of heavenly beings (Exodus 20:3-5) – "You shall not make for yourself an idol, whether in the form of anything that is in heaven above, or that is on the earth beneath, or that is in the water under the earth. You shall not bow down to them or worship them; for I the Lord your God am a jealous God" (NRSVA). This injunction should probably have prevented artists creating such contradictory images of angels. Then again, Moses later said that God had commanded him to place two angelic images of cherubim on top of the Ark of the Covenant, which the Christian church has traditionally taken to mean that artists can create such religious icons, but only as long as they venerate the one true God, instead of other, pagan gods.)

The Male Victims of War Rape

Although we commonly associate war rape as a crime with only female victims, there is a growing body of evidence that men also are often the victims of war rape. For instance, Will Storr wrote an article in *The Guardian* in 2011 called *The Rape of Men: the Darkest Secret of War*, which he based on Lara Stemple's 2009 academic article *Male Rape and Human Rights*. According to Stemple and Storr, there are male victims of war rape throughout the world, in many cultures. However, one example that stood out to me from Storr's article was that of male war rape victims in Uganda:

In Uganda, survivors are at risk of arrest by police, as they are likely to assume that they're gay – a crime in this country and in 38 of the 53 African nations. They will probably be ostracised by friends, rejected by family and turned away by the UN and the myriad international NGOs that are equipped, trained and ready to help women. They are wounded, isolated and in danger.

This struck a chord with me, because some of the most outspoken opponents to the Church of England blessing same sex marriages have been conservative African Christian leaders, such as Archbishop Ntagali of Uganda.

*

African Opposition to Same Sex Marriage Stoked by American Evangelicals

In January 2014, the Archbishops of Canterbury and York wrote an open letter to all Anglican communities reminding them of the Dromantine Communiqué of 2005, which stated that:

> The victimisation or diminishment of human beings whose affections happen to be ordered towards people of the same sex is anathema to us. We assure homosexual people that they are children of God, loved and valued by Him and deserving the best we can give - pastoral care and friendship.

The Archbishops of Canterbury and York wrote this in the light of the recent passing of punitive anti-homosexual laws in Nigeria and Uganda. Archbishop Ntagali's response to the open letter contained an explicit threat that the Church of Uganda would leave the Anglican Communion if the Church of England ever approved the blessing of or conducting of same sex marriages. To complicate matters, in January 2010, *The New York Times* reported that the visit to Uganda of three conservative evangelical American Christians with an anti-LGBT agenda in 2009 helped stoked that country's push towards outlawing homosexuality. (You can find an excellent account of this incident in *Uganda, United States and Europe: The Anti-Homosexual Law* of 2014 by M. L. Stevens.)

The Taboo against Homosexuality in Patriarchal Cultures

The taboo against homosexuality in patriarchal societies throughout the world contributes greatly to the under-reporting of instances of male victims of war rape. As described in Will Storr's article in *The Guardian*, because homosexuality is taboo in such patriarchal societies, this often means that male rape is not reported by the victims, because they are afraid that the authorities will punish them even further, by, say, jailing them for being homosexual. In a society where homosexuality is so taboo, male soldiers subjecting their male prisoners to rape often do so because this is the most degrading punishment that they can think of for their enemies, and because they know that their victims will never report the crime, for fear of being stigmatised further. Male victims of war rape in patriarchal cultures where men feel that they have to always appear virile and manly, often find that their own family members and wives shun them when they discover that they have been victims of this crime. International charities and NGOs are so focussed on supporting the female victims of war rape that they do not have the resources or inclination to help male victims of war rape, according to Storr and Stemple.

Sodom as an Early Example of Historical War Rape

Although the story of Sodom initially appears as an atypical example of an atrocity that has never been repeated in human history, we can now perhaps regard it instead as the most famous example of a heinous crime that has all too often gone unpunished, and one that is still prevalent in the world today. Not that this will be of any comfort to contemporary male victims of war rape.

The Sodomite Threat of Sexual Violence

In many ways, the story of Sodom and Gomorrah is like that of Noah's Ark, in that people view a major environmental disaster as God's punishment for humanity's sins, i.e., the Sodomites must have been really evil if God saw fit to destroy their city with fire and sulphur. As I have mentioned above, many conservative Christian commentators have seen Sodom's sin as homosexuality, and it was their vile prejudice that led to 'sodomy' becoming the legal term for 'homosexuality'. However, after a close re-examination of the text, I think Sodom's sin is more clearly defined as being that of rape. So when I read denunciations of sodomy in a Biblical translation, such as in the New Revised Standard Version, then I read it as condemning rape, rather than homosexuality. (This is why I choose to read the New Revised Standard Version of the Bible, as I am much more comfortable reading 1 Corinthians 6:9 and 1 Timothy 1:10 as prohibiting rape, rather than homosexuality. The New Revised Standard Version is also translated into modern English, so making it very readable.)

*

Sodom's Sin as Gross Inhospitality

Other Biblical authors that refer to Sodom's grave sin do not mention homosexuality; instead, they see Sodom's sin as gross inhospitality. This was certainly the view of Ezekiel (16:49-50):

This was the guilt of your sister Sodom: she and her daughters had pride, excess of food, and prosperous ease, but did not aid the poor and needy. They were haughty, and did abominable things before me; therefore I removed them when I saw it. (NRSVA)

This is what Jesus also thought of Sodom and Gomorrah (Matthew 10:14-15):

If anyone will not welcome you or listen to your words, shake off the dust from your feet as you leave that house or town. Truly I tell you, it will be more tolerable for the land of Sodom and Gomorrah on the day of judgement than for that town. (NRSVA)

Jesus used Sodom and Gomorrah here to equate these cities to any place that would not welcome his disciples.

The Sexual Immorality of Lot's Daughters in the Wake of the Destruction of Sodom

Indeed, if Sodom and Gomorrah's main sin was that of sexual immorality, then this is a lesson that Lot's own daughters have not taken on board. For, in the aftermath of Sodom and Gomorrah's destruction, Lot's daughters plied their father with drink, so that they could make Lot sire children without realising who he was sleeping with. This is a rather extraordinary conclusion to the tale of Sodom, and if true, can only be explained away by Lot's daughters believing that they were in a survival situation, like a plane crash in the Andes that necessitates survivors cannibalising the dead. (The fiancés of Lot's daughters died in Sodom's desolation.) Since Lot and his daughters saw Sodom's destruction, then one can only think that they were suffering from post-traumatic stress, and that this contributed to the way that Lot's daughters behaved. Moses later banned the offspring of Lot's daughters (the Ammonites and the Moabites) from attending the Lord's Assembly of the Israelites, probably partly due to their incestuous, illegitimate origins, although Moses stated that their banishment was mainly to do with their inhospitality to the Israelites during their exodus. While most liberal Christians do not believe homosexuality is a sin, they do still frown upon incest and adultery as forms of sexual immorality.

The Tribe of Benjamin's Inhospitality

There is another incident in the Bible that is similar in tone to Sodom and Gomorrah's destruction, and that is the one that precipitated the Battle of Gibeah. The story begins with a Levite following his concubine to her father's home after she has run away from him. The Levite manages to charm his concubine (and perhaps more importantly, her father), so that she agrees to return home with him. However, the concubine's father is so keen on entertaining his guest that he delays their departure time. So much so, that the Levite, his concubine and his servant, have to seek shelter overnight on their way home. The servant suggests that they stay in Jerusalem, but the Levite is not keen on this, as Jerusalem is a Jebusite city (this was before the capture of Jerusalem by the Israelites). So, the Levite chooses to stay in Gibeah instead, as this is the territory of the Israelite tribe of Benjamin. However, nobody gives them shelter until an old man appears on the horizon. This old man is from Ephraim, rather than the tribe of Benjamin, which may explain why he appears to have better manners than the local inhabitants. In this way, the old man is rather like Lot, who, although he lived in Sodom, was not a native Sodomite. This is the story in Judges 19:22-28:

> While they were enjoying themselves, the men of the city, a depraved lot, surrounded the house, and started pounding on the door. They said to the old man, the master of the house, 'Bring out the man who came into your house, so that we may have intercourse with him.' And the man, the master of the house, went out to them and said to them, 'No, my brothers, do not act so wickedly. Since this man is my guest, do not do this vile thing. Here are my virgin daughter and his concubine; let me bring them out now. Ravish them and do whatever you want to them; but against this man do

44

not do such a vile thing.' But the men would not listen to him. So the man seized his concubine, and put her out to them. They wantonly raped her, and abused her all through the night until the morning. And as the dawn began to break, they let her go. As morning appeared, the woman came and fell down at the door of the man's house where her master was, until it was light.

In the morning her master got up, opened the doors of the house, and when he went out to go on his way, there was his concubine lying at the door of the house, with her hands on the threshold. 'Get up,' he said to her, 'we are going.' But there was no answer. (NRSVA)

Again in this story, like Sodom, there is the rather bizarre element that the owner of the house offers up the women of the house to the mob (his own daughter and the concubine), rather than the male guest that the mob wants to rape and humiliate. As I wrote above, the Victorians were a very patriarchal society; however, Victorian men did have an idealised image of womanhood, 'the angel of the house', whose virtue they would vigorously defend. Unfortunately, unlike at Sodom, there are no angels in the house here, only the householder's virgin daughter and the concubine. And it is rather telling that the Levite chooses to expel his concubine to face the mob's violence, instead of the virgin daughter, who still has some capital as a future wife. As I have written before, this early Israelite culture was very evidently extremely patriarchal, where men saw women as being little more than possessions. So, although the Levite is rightly angered by the gang rape of his concubine, and her death as a result of this brutality, the Levite is very much to blame for her death also. Indeed, the very fact that this story is so explicit about the unsavoury nature of the Levite, makes one think that there is more than a little grain of truth in it, and that this must have been a real incident. (Some commentators believe that this story is a piece of propaganda by King David to defend him punishing the tribe of his predecessor, King Saul, who was a Benjamite.) Certainly the concubine was correct in her belief that the Levite was no good for her, when she originally ran away from him. The Levite unquestionably talks to her lifeless body as he would have done to a dog. (Incidentally, although the concubine is not the Levite's wife, the Levite is not condemned for having extramarital or adulterous sex with her, for it was

45

customary for Israelite men to have concubines - one of this patriarchal culture's many double standards.)

Moses' Patriarchal Rape Laws

Moses' laws do prohibit rape, in the same part of Deuteronomy that condemns transvestism (Deuteronomy 22:23-29):

> If there is a young woman, a virgin already engaged to be married, and a man meets her in the town and lies with her, you shall bring both of them to the gate of that town and stone them to death, the young woman because she did not cry for help in the town and the man because he violated his neighbour's wife. So you shall purge the evil from your midst.
>
> But if the man meets the engaged woman in the open country, and the man seizes her and lies with her, then only the man who lay with her shall die. You shall do nothing to the young woman; the young woman has not committed an offence punishable by death, because this case is like that of someone who attacks and murders a neighbour. Since he found her in the open country, the engaged woman may have cried for help, but there was no one to rescue her.
>
> If a man meets a virgin who is not engaged, and seizes her and lies with her, and they are caught in the act, the man who lay with her shall give fifty shekels of silver to the young woman's father, and she shall become his wife. Because he violated her he shall not be permitted to divorce her as long as he lives. (NRSVA)

We see in the above passages some very patriarchal stereotypes about rape. In the first instance, the woman in the town faces the death penalty because she did not cry out for help. It is a sad indictment of current criminal justice systems that rape victims are still often asked in court: "Why didn't you cry out for help?" Beyond this, one must point that Moses' society clearly regarded women as being the property of their fathers or their fiancés, especially since the penalty prescribed for the rapist of a virgin is merely a financial one, to pay her father a dowry. Our sensibilities have changed for the

46

better, for such a disgusting arrangement (the rapist marrying his victim) would be obviously be unpalatable to the victim and her family today. Again, this law of Moses reinforces the unsavoury fact that women were just treated as the property of their husbands and fathers in Moses' day. Even the most conservative of Christians must admit that there are few, if any, of Moses' punishments that they follow today, for good reason, despite their being part of Scripture; so this should make conservative Christians pause for thought when they insist on promulgating the sentiments of Moses' unjust laws against gay people.

Going back to the Gibeah story, so angered is the Levite by the concubine's death that he then takes the extraordinary step of cutting up her body into twelve pieces to send to the twelve tribes of Israel as evidence of the tribe of Benjamin's gross inhospitality. (Presumably the mob beat her body black and blue. The Levite's action is a rather primitive precursor to forensic post-mortem photographic evidence.) However, one cannot be sure whether the Levite detests the tribe of Benjamin's destruction of his 'property' more than their inhospitality to him. Such is the tribe of Benjamin's rampant territoriality (like that of the Sodomites) that their actions are more akin to war rape, even though it occurs outside of warfare (then again, the Israelites were so angered by this incident that they waged war against the tribe of Benjamin). I must repeat that the crime that the Israelites believe that the tribe of Benjamin had committed was not that of homosexuality (or bisexuality when they raped the concubine instead of the Levite), but that of inhospitality, of not treating foreigners and travellers with respect, and not providing shelter for them.

The Modern Inhospitable Treatment of Gay People

The Archbishop of Canterbury recently said in a LBC radio interview that if the Church of England were to conduct same sex marriages, then this could put the lives of Christians in Africa in great peril. The Archbishop spoke of witnessing a mass grave of Christians in Africa, who were reportedly murdered by the local community who feared that these Christians would force them into homosexuality. Supporters of the Archbishop's stance argue that he was not saying that the Church of England should never adopt same sex marriage for fear of similar mass murders; rather that the Archbishop was stating that there are very deeply entrenched views on both sides of the debate, and that he has to respect the African churches' opposition to homosexuality, since homosexuality is so widely condemned in the Bible. Hopefully my re-reading of the passages in the Bible that have been traditionally viewed by conservative Christians as being divine punishment for homosexuality will gradually help to eradicate this historic prejudice and injustice. In the meantime, I very much support the Church of England's appeal to the African Churches to actively work to repeal their countries' punitive laws against homosexuality. I also call for the UK Immigration officials display far more hospitality to LGBT people fleeing such persecution; it is disappointing to hear that the British Home Secretary has had to censure Immigration officials for interrogating LGBT asylum seekers about their sexual habits, and so humiliating even further those who have already suffered so much.

The Roman Catholic Sexual Abuse Cases Compared to Sodom and Gibeah

However, this issue of rape and inhospitable abuse of power is not one that is just confined to impoverished 'Third World' countries, for such disgusting incidents occur in the West also. I am referring here to the Roman Catholic sex abuse cases. It is outrageous that in the past, the Roman Catholic Church commonly reacted to abuse allegations by moving the offending priest to another parish, where they were free to commit such vile acts again. The victims of these priests were in their care, and were guests in the House of the Lord, and so these assaults against them were acts of gross inhospitality, as bad as that at Sodom and Gibeah. It matters not whether these assaults happened on church soil, the principle is the same, for these victims were in the care of their priest when he abused them. And yet, the Roman Catholic Church has seemed more concerned about looking after their priests than their victims, their guests in the House of the Lord. By comparing the Roman Catholic sex abuse cases with the Biblical examples of Sodom and Gibeah, I hope to finally make the Holy See understand why there is such anger against the Roman Catholic Church for their mishandling of these crimes. The Lord punished Sodom's rapacious mob by destroying them with fire and sulphur, and the Israelites decimated the tribe of Benjamin as punishment for gang rape and murder. And yet still the Roman Catholic Church refuses to fully confess to its participation in similar crimes, despite the public's very great anger against them.

The Roman Catholic Church has to Fully Confess its Role in Hiding Priests' Sexual Abuses

During my writing of this book, Pope Francis has apologised for these Roman Catholic abuse cases, saying that they were "moral damage carried out by men of the Church". He went on to "personally ask for forgiveness for the damage [some priests] have done for having sexually abused children", and he said that sanctions would be imposed against guilty priests. Few of the victims of these priests will ever forgive them, or the Roman Catholic Church for the manner in which they dealt with these abuses; this is something that the Roman Catholic Church will have to accept.

The Roman Catholic Church has to Hand Priests Guilty of Sexual Abuses to the Civil Authorities

However, I doubt whether society will ever fully forgive the Roman Catholic Church unless it completely discloses how they dealt with these guilty priests, and until they finally turn all these priests over to the civil law courts. "Render therefore unto Caesar the things which are Caesar's; and unto God the things that are God's", as our Lord Jesus Christ himself commanded (Matthew 22:21). I am not saying that the Roman Catholic Church should abandon these priests entirely; no, they should give them the same pastoral care that they would give to any other repentant sinner convicted in civil courts for such crimes.

Confession is an Empty Sacrament if it Allows Repetition of Sin

If a priest has used the ritual of confession to admit his crime to his bishop or any other clergy, then the only fitting penance for such a priest will be to repeat his confession to the police within 24 hours. If the guilty priest does not present himself to the authorities within 24 hours, then he will have violated the confession's sanctity himself, meaning that the clergy to whom he had confessed would have no option but to tell the authorities of the confession.

There are those who would say that confession is a holy sacrament; I say to these people that they are blinder than the scribes and the Pharisees of old if they think that following a ritual that could lead to evil's repetition will ever bring them to salvation. In the past, the Roman Catholic Church used to send clergy guilty of sexual abuses away to psychiatric clinics in the hope that they could be 'cured'. However, we now know that many paedophiles find it difficult, if not impossible, to completely reform. Therefore, a priest that is guilty of sexual abuse must always be defrocked; to do anything else would be a complete dereliction of the Roman Catholic Church's duty of care to their community and parishioners. Of course, if someone accuses a priest of abuse, and the priest proclaims their innocence, then the Roman Catholic Church should give legal support to such clergy in court. If the priest has declared their guilt in the confession box, then it is imperative that the guilty priest and the Roman Catholic Church must openly confess this sin in court.

Why the Church No Longer Needs to Fear Civil Law

As I have previously mentioned, Paul wrote to the Corinthian Church, telling them not to take their disputes to civil courts (1 Corinthians 6:1-8):

> When any of you has a grievance against another, do you dare to take it to court before the unrighteous, instead of taking it before the saints? Do you not know that the saints will judge the world? And if the world is to be judged by you, are you incompetent to try trivial cases? Do you not know that we are to judge angels—to say nothing of ordinary matters? If you have ordinary cases, then, do you appoint as judges those who have no standing in the church? I say this to your shame. Can it be that there is no one among you wise enough to decide between one believer and another, but a believer goes to court against a believer—and before unbelievers at that?

> In fact, to have lawsuits at all with one another is already a defeat for you. Why not rather be wronged? Why not rather be defrauded? But you yourselves wrong and defraud—and believers at that. (NRSVA)

At the time when Paul wrote the above passage, the young church was still very vulnerable to attack by outside forces, and this is another instance of him being overprotective towards nascent Christianity. So Christians taking disputes against one another to civil courts could very well have brought the young church into disrepute. However, when Christianity is the state religion of so many countries around the world two thousand years later, such protection is no longer needed. Indeed, the Roman Catholic Church now is in disrepute precisely because it has not turned priests guilty of sexual abuse over to the civil courts. Again, I am sure that Paul himself would have shocked to discover that the Roman Catholic Church is still using his words from over two thousand years ago to hide the truth about sex abuse cases. Besides, Paul intended to prevent disputes between members of the congregation in the above letter; he did not mean it to cover instances where clergy (in positions of power) abused members of their congregation or community. According to the 1913 *Catholic Encyclopedia*, the following is the justification for not turning clergy over to the civil courts:

The Church could not permit her clergy to be judged by laymen; it would be utterly unbecoming for persons of superior dignity to submit themselves to their inferiors for judgment. The clergy, therefore, were exempt from civil jurisdiction, and this ancient rule was sanctioned by custom and confirmed by written laws. On this point the Church has always taken a firm stand; concessions have been wrung from her only where greater evils were to be avoided.

Looking beyond the inherent arrogance of the first sentence, one can only point out that sex abuse cases must obviously be one of those areas where "greater evils" will occur if guilty priests do not face trial before civil courts. Indeed, many of the priests that the Roman Catholic authorities dealt with inadequately went on to abuse more children in the new parishes that their bishops moved them into. While one deplores the despicable murder of Thomas Becket, the Archbishop of Canterbury in 1170, one has to admit that King Henry II was right to demand that the church hand over lay clergy found guilty of serious crimes in ecclesiastical courts to the civil courts, where they would receive far more severe sentences. Unfortunately, Thomas Becket refused to compromise on this issue, which meant that many of these lay clergy in England went on to commit many more serious crimes. Like St.

Paul, Thomas Becket suffered greatly on behalf of Christianity, but the call of both these saints for the church not to hand over clergy to the civil courts caused a great deal more harm to later victims of abuses at the hands of their priests.

The Roman Catholic Church Must be More Transparent When Dealing with Sexual Abuse Cases

The Pope has recently complained that no other institution has done more to combat the sexual abuse of children. He has also said, "The Catholic Church is perhaps the only public institution to have acted with transparency and responsibility… Yet the Church is the only one to have been attacked." However, given that there are more than 1.2 billion Catholics worldwide, it is not surprising that the Roman Catholic Church has faced so many accusations of child sexual abuse, since it is one of the largest institutions in the world. I fully accept that a Roman Catholic priest is no more likely to become a child sex abuser than anyone else. What is at issue here is how the Roman Catholic Church has historically dealt with accusations of child sexual abuse, and how it deals with this most grievous of sins. The Pope is blinder than the scribes and Pharisees of old if he believes that the Roman Catholic Church has acted with "transparency" in child sex abuse cases, as the Holy See's lack of transparency is why the public is so upset by its lacklustre response to these crimes. I say this to the Pope; you must, with all humility, thoroughly and openly confess how the Roman Catholic Church has dealt with all accusations of sexual abuse against children, and give the police the names of all the accused clergy that the civil authorities have yet to prosecute. This is the only way that innocent clergy can clear their names, and for the civil authorities to effectively punish guilty clergy. For it is glaringly obvious now that there is a huge conflict of interest in the Roman Catholic Church trying to resolve these cases itself, without recourse to criminal law. The Vatican announced in 2013 that it would sct up a commission to guarantee the safeguarding of minors within the Roman Catholic Church, which according to the BBC, would include "taking criminal action against offenders… and defining the civil and clerical duties within the Church". This sounds very much like a step in the right direction; however, only the complete openness that I have called for, along with the arrest and prosecution of offending priests, will be enough to satisfy the public that the Roman Catholic Church has finally come to terms with these grievous abuses.

Conservative Christians' False Accusation that Liberal Christians Tolerate Sexual Immorality

Along with the rather ridiculous complaint that the Roman Catholic Church is being unfairly criticised for its safeguarding of children in comparison to other institutions, such as private schools (that obviously are not one of the largest organisations in the world, and a religious one at that), several conservative apologists for the Holy See's approach accuse their critics of being hypocrites for their acceptance of 'sexual immorality'. These are some of the views of Jeffrey A. Mirus on the Roman Catholic child sex abuse controversy:

So, if your view of the results of the sex abuse scandal is that the Church is getting exactly what it deserves, I would be sympathetic... if those of us who point out the large role homosexuality has played in this abuse were not excoriated for daring to suggest there is anything disordered about homosexuality... So the first lesson of the abuse scandal is that the extent to which the Church is under attack is determined in large part by the hatred many people feel for the Church's stance *against* the prevailing sins of the surrounding culture, including sexual sins. Surely far more people have been discomfited by the Church's insistence on traditional sexual morality than have suffered at the hands of those priests and bishops who have failed to live the gospel in this particular way. But the secular world regards insistence on sexual morality as another form of abuse, doesn't it?

The following quote from the Catholic magazine *Crisis* from 2002 also despicably associates homosexuality with paedophilia (the typographical errors come from the original):

In 1975, the Church issued another document called "Declaration on Certain Questions Concerning Sexual Ethics" (written by Joseph Cardinal Joseph Ratzinger) that explicitly addressed, among other issues, the problem of homosexuality among priests. Both the 1967 and 1975 documents addressed kinds of sexual deviancy, including pedophilia and

53

ephebophilia, that are is especially prevalent among homosexuals.

Some Conservative Christians Wrongly Equate Homosexuality with Paedophilia

These two conservative Catholic commentators ignorantly and disgracefully associate paedophilia with homosexuality without realizing that there is a massive ethical difference between a sexual act committed by two consenting adults, and the sexual abuse of a child. These ignorant conservative Catholic apologists make this association because homosexuality is so widely condemned in the Bible, while paedophilia is not, and so these idiots have the gall to accuse us of hypocrisy because we fight to end the unjust Biblical persecution against homosexuality. In the idiot minds of these conservative Catholic apologists, the prohibition against homosexuality is the 'closest' that they can find to an injunction against paedophilia in the Bible, despite the fact that many of victims of these male priests were and are female. *Besides, it is simply not true that liberal Christians tolerate sexual immorality: we oppose it just as much as conservative Christians. It's just that liberal Christians have a different definition of sexual immorality than conservative Christians, for we liberals, while agreeing with conservatives that incest, adultery, paedophilia and rape are sins, vehemently argue that homosexuality is not a sin.*

The Lack of a Condemnation of Paedophilia in the Bible

If only Moses and St. Paul had condemned paedophilia instead of homosexuality! Then maybe the Roman Catholic Church would have acted far more responsibly over accusations of child sexual abuse, and the suffering of many thousands of abuse victims would have prevented, along with the unjust persecution of gay people. However, if nothing else, the lack of a proscription against paedophilia is more evidence (if any be needed) that the people of the Bible lived in a very different world from our own. In Biblical times, there was no legal age of consent, and people married at a younger age, often at the onset of puberty, or even younger, so there was no real concept of paedophilia. This is mainly because mortality rates were higher (i.e., people died younger than they do in the affluent West today, and so they married younger). We now afford children far better protection than they had in the past, and we should keep it this way. We no longer treat women and girls especially as property, as was the custom in Biblical times, and this is mainly due to the recent rise of feminism, along with the teachings of our Lord Jesus Christ. Some commentators regard Matthew 18:6 as being Jesus' injunction against paedophilia:

> At that time the disciples came to Jesus and asked, 'Who is the greatest in the kingdom of heaven?' He called a child, whom he put among them, and said, 'Truly I tell you, unless you change and become like children, you will never enter the kingdom of heaven. Whoever becomes humble like this child is the greatest in the kingdom of heaven. Whoever welcomes one such child in my name welcomes me.

> 'If any of you put a stumbling-block before one of these little ones who believe in me, it would be better for you if a great millstone were fastened around your neck and you were drowned in the depth of the sea...' (Matthew 18:1-6, NRSVA)

However, I do not think that the above is the Lord's condemnation of paedophilia, as some Biblical editors translate the above passage as an injunction against leading little ones into temptation and sin, and since a child that suffers sexual abuse is obviously not a sinner, it would be monstrous for anyone to claim otherwise. Vigilantes are also likely to misread the above passage, and could take it as the justification to kill a suspected paedophile, although obviously there is little opportunity for anyone to get their hands on a millstone today. So in the above passage, Jesus was actually sternly warning anyone thinking of leading any of his flock astray that they would not receive salvation, instead of condemning paedophilia.

Paul's Rejection of the Veil of Moses and the Ministry of Death

I have been quite critical of St. Paul in this book, because at times, his writing harks back to his patriarchal heritage as a Pharisee, and it seems that he has forgotten the light that our Lord Jesus Christ brought to bear on our lives. However, as I have mentioned before, there are passages where Paul's teaching of the Gospel is sublime, such as 2 Corinthians 3, where he discusses the ministry of Christ's new covenant:

Are we beginning to commend ourselves again? Surely we do not need, as some do, letters of recommendation to you or from you, do we? You yourselves are our letter, written on our hearts, to be known and read by all; and you show that you are a letter of Christ, prepared by us, written not with ink but with the Spirit of the living God, not on tablets of stone but on tablets of human hearts.

Such is the confidence that we have through Christ towards God. Not that we are competent of ourselves to claim anything as coming from us; our competence is from God, who has made us competent to be ministers of a new covenant, not of letter but of spirit; for the letter kills, but the Spirit gives life.

Now if the ministry of death, chiseled in letters on stone tablets, came in glory so that the people of Israel could not gaze at Moses' face because of the glory of his face, a glory now set aside, how much more will the ministry of the Spirit come in glory? For if there was glory in the ministry of condemnation, much more does the ministry of justification abound in glory! Indeed, what once had glory has lost its glory because of the greater glory; for if what was set aside came through glory, much more has the permanent come in glory!

Since, then, we have such a hope, we act with great boldness, not like Moses, who put a veil over his face to keep the people of Israel from gazing at the end of the glory that was being set aside. But their minds were hardened. Indeed, to this very day, when they hear the reading of the old covenant, that same veil is still there, since only in Christ is it set aside. Indeed, to this very day whenever Moses is read, a veil lies over their minds; but when one turns to the Lord, the veil is removed. Now the Lord is the Spirit, and where the Spirit of the Lord is, there is freedom. And all of us, with unveiled faces, seeing the glory of the Lord as though reflected in a mirror, are being transformed into the same image from one degree of glory to another; for this comes from the Lord, the Spirit. (NRSVA)

The above passage is a very apt summary of this book, where Paul argues (like me) that our Lord Jesus Christ reformed the Ten Commandments ("chiseled in letters on stone tablets") and all the laws of Moses, by bringing eternal life instead of the death penalty for 'crimes' such as homosexuality. Indeed, for those conservative Christians who still believe that Moses' condemnation of homosexuality stands today, "that same veil is still there". These conservative Christians forget to turn to the Lord on issues such as homosexuality, for in their condemnations of gay people, it is quite clear that they have not removed the veil of the old covenant. This is very understandable – "Indeed, to this very day whenever Moses is read, a veil lies over their minds" – and this veil is so dark and overwhelming that it even obscures St. Paul's vision when he prohibits homosexuality. Conservative Christians must remove the veil of the old covenant by turning to the Lord, as Paul writes, and forget the old Mosaic condemnations of homosexuality, such as Leviticus (20.13): "If a man lies with a male as with a woman, both of them have committed an abomination; they shall be put to death; their blood is upon them". Indeed, I think that Pope Francis was thinking of the above passage when he addressed the conservatives attending the 2014 Catholic Family Synod, telling them to avoid "a temptation to hostile inflexibility, that is, wanting to close oneself within the written word, (the letter) and not allowing oneself to be surprised by God, by the God of surprises, (the spirit); within the law, within the certitude of what we know and not of what we still need to learn and to achieve. From the time of Christ, it is the temptation of the zealous, of the scrupulous, of the solicitous and of the so-called – today – 'traditionalists'."

The Holy Spirit Moves us to Compassion

As the Pope above refers to the "God of surprises", it does indeed seem as though the Lord our God has changed His mind on homosexuality. The Holy Spirit has moved many of us to ever more compassion, so that we no longer see homosexuality as a crime. As I have pointed out in this book, although most of the Ten Commandments are universal, we apply few, if any, of Moses' laws to the letter today. Indeed, the Holy Spirit has changed our values in many ways since the times of the Israelites, so that men no longer see women and children as property, which has given rise to women's equality to

57

men through the rise of feminism, and has provided greater safeguarding for our children. We no longer offer to sacrifice our children to the wolves of the night, as the old man from Ephraim and Lot were all too willing to do. This is why we now have parliaments and synods, as we no longer write our laws on stone, but form and refine them through the light of the Holy Spirit. I pray that the Holy Spirit will in time remove the veil of the old covenant from all people, so that they will see that, like slavery, homophobia is a sin that we should consign to history.

Three: Love Your Neighbour as Yourself
The Parable of the Prodigal Son – a model for Christian unity over the issue of same sex marriage

The Parable of the Prodigal Son Still Resonates

When I first came across the Parable of the Prodigal Son as a child, my feelings were that the story was very unfair (Luke 15:11-32):

Jesus said, 'There was a man who had two sons. The younger of them said to his father, "Father, give me the share of the property that will belong to me." So he divided his property between them. A few days later the younger son gathered all he had and travelled to a distant country, and there he squandered his property in dissolute living. When he had spent everything, a severe famine took place throughout that country, and he began to be in need. So he went and hired himself out to one of the citizens of that country, who sent him to his fields to feed the pigs. He would gladly have filled himself with the pods that the pigs were eating; and no one gave him anything. But when he came to himself he said, "How many of my father's hired hands have bread enough and to spare, but here I am dying of hunger! I will get up and go to my father, and I will say to him, 'Father, I have sinned against heaven and before you; I am no longer worthy to be called your son; treat me like one of your hired hands.'" So he set off and went to his father. But while he was still far off, his father saw him and was filled with compassion; he ran and put his arms around him and kissed him. Then the son said to him, "Father, I have sinned against heaven and before you; I am no longer worthy to be called your son." But the father said to his slaves, "Quickly, bring out a robe—the best one—and put it on him; put a ring on his finger and sandals on his feet. And get the fatted calf and kill it, and let us eat and celebrate; for this son of mine was dead and is alive again; he was lost and is found!" And they began to celebrate.

'Now his elder son was in the field; and when he came and approached the house, he heard music and dancing. He called one of the slaves and asked what was going on. He replied, "Your brother has come, and your father has killed the fatted calf, because he has got him back safe and sound."

Then he became angry and refused to go in. His father came out and began to plead with him. But he answered his father, "Listen! For all these years I have been working like a slave for you, and I have never disobeyed your command; yet you have never given me even a young goat so that I might celebrate with my friends. But when this son of yours came back, who has devoured your property with prostitutes, you killed the fatted calf for him!" Then the father said to him, "Son, you are always with me, and all that is mine is yours. But we had to celebrate and rejoice, because this brother of yours was dead and has come to life; he was lost and has been found."'(NRSVA)

Indeed, even to this day, part of me is resentful when I read the Parable of the Prodigal Son. If I have been a good and faithful son in every way, then how can it be justice when my Father makes such a fuss over the return home of my wastrel younger brother? Surely I deserve far more rewards, such as the best clothes and food, than a younger brother that has never contributed anything? Such is the power of the Parable of the Prodigal Son that it still strikes a chord in me to this very day. Our Lord Jesus Christ was very wise to impart his lessons via parables and metaphors, since these devices make His teachings alive and relevant to every generation that puzzles and debates over what He truly meant, much as His audiences did in New Testament times. This means that Jesus could deal with timeless, universal themes and issues far more effectively than say, the more direct and to the point style of St. Paul. I think that the Parable of the Prodigal Son is a very apt analogy for the divisions in Christian churches over the issue of same sex marriage. The older son of the story is, for me, very akin to conservative Christians, while conservative Christians probably regard those people who want churches to conduct same sex marriage services as being very much like the improvident younger son.

The Parable of the Prodigal Son's Relevance to the Same Sex Marriage Debate

As I have written before, the Holy Spirit has moved me and the great majority of the British public into accepting homosexuality. Since we do not believe homosexual acts are sinful, we, unlike conservative Christians, do not ask gay people to repent for their sexual behaviour like the prodigal son does for his. For instance, we argue that it is discriminatory that the Church of England requires celibacy from homosexual clergy, while their heterosexual colleagues do not face this restriction. (Such discrimination, as I have written before, goes against James the Just's injunction that Christians be impartial when dealing with one another: "You do well if you really fulfil the royal law according to the scripture, 'You shall love your neighbour as yourself.' But if you show partiality, you commit sin and are convicted by the law as transgressors" [The Letter of James, 2:8-9]). So, in this analogy, like the Father, we welcome homosexual clergy, and celebrate that God has called them to evangelise the Gospel in the House of the Lord, and that they do so despite opposition from conservative Christians. Likewise, I argue that if a same sex couple feels called to celebrate their union in church then the Church of England and other ecclesiastical bodies should welcome them. Rather than denigrating marriage, the wish of same sex couples to wed reinforces and enhances marriage. The Holy Spirit has removed the veil of bigotry from legislators, who have passed laws internationally that enable same sex partners to enjoy a family life and to raise children. It is therefore natural that same sex couples should want to mark their union by embracing marriage, in order that they may deliver ever more stability to their families. We should celebrate, instead of discriminate against, same sex couples that feel called to marry in church, for by so doing, they graciously and publicly forgive three thousand years of persecution, and so evangelise the Gospel. That is why we must finally hold wedding feasts for our prodigal sons and daughters, to rejoice in their return to the House of the Lord! This is why the Father commands his servants (the clergy) to put a ring upon the hand of the prodigal son, and to dress him in the best robes, as befits a wedding feast. (The hosts of a wedding feast would slaughter their fattened calves to feed their guests, as Jesus related in the Parable of the Wedding Banquet [Matthew 22:4], so this also fits in neatly into my wedding analogy.) Note that the Heavenly Father in the parable is unquestioning in his forgiveness of the prodigal son, and that He does not ask the prodigal son to debase himself in any way, as He interrupts his son before he can offer service as a hired hand.

*

We Should Rename this 'The Parable of the Lost Son and the Self-Righteous Son'

The Parable of the Prodigal Son has some alternative names, such as 'Lost Son', 'the Running Father' and 'the Loving Father'. However, I think that a better name would be 'The Parable of the Lost Son and the Self-Righteous Son'. Alternatively, 'The Parable of the Liberal Son and the Conservative Son' makes for a snappier title and very much fits the theme of this book! For far too long, our focus has been on the younger son, because he is the more obvious sinner. However, the older son sins too, by refusing to offer the same unquestioning forgiveness and hospitality to his younger brother that his Heavenly Father does. The older son represents the Pharisees, who made a point of publicly and self-righteously following all the rituals and sacrifices laid down to them by God to the letter (i.e., doing everything by the Book), all the while despising brethren like the prodigal son who lacked the discipline to do the same. Our Lord Jesus Christ did not speak out against homosexuals, but he often condemned the Pharisees for their hypocrisy. Conservative Christians focus on the prodigal son, because he is a good example of all the ills of the world, showing how decadent sinners can come back into the fold if they repent, so making conservative Christians feel good about their forgiving nature. Yet gay people do not want your condescending compassion; no, they ask for nothing less than your acceptance and respect for who they are.

Conservative Christians are the Modern Pharisees

Conservative Christians, when reading this story, will no doubt recognise that Jesus was referring to the Pharisees via the metaphor of the older, jealous son. However, since the Pharisees are long dead, a part of history, conservative Christians lose sight of the older son's sin, because they think that the Pharisees are no longer relevant to today's world. But I say to conservative Christians, "Go look in a mirror!" For if you do, if you truly look, and if the Holy Spirit lifts this wedding veil from before your eyes, then you will see a Pharisee looking back at you. For instance, I could not have published this book with Xulon Press, the Christian self-publishing company, as arguing for same sex marriage contravenes the 'statement of faith' that was on their website as I wrote this book:

Most online and on-demand publishers gladly accept books written by authors who degrade the gospel. In fact, some of the leading on-demand publishers accept manuscripts dealing with the occult, New Age belief, pornography, homosexuality, and other subjects condemned by Scripture.

Conservative Christians focus too much on the letter of the law, while forgetting the life-enhancing spirit of the new covenant of Jesus. For instance, one of conservative Christianity's main objections to same sex marriage (as I have discussed before) is that it does not fit their definition of wedlock, which they based upon the words of our Lord Jesus Christ (Matthew 19:3-7):

Some Pharisees came to him, and to test him they asked, 'Is it lawful for a man to divorce his wife for any cause?' He answered, 'Have you not read that the one who made them at the beginning "made them male and female", and said, "For this reason a man shall leave his father and mother and be joined to his wife, and the two shall become one flesh"? So they are no longer two, but one flesh. Therefore what God has joined together, let no one separate.' (NRSVA)

As I have argued before, what our Lord Jesus Christ was saying here was not that the participants in marriage can only be male and female, but that His disciples should commit to a wife for life, and not discard their wife on a whim. So, Jesus' main point here was to command His disciples and followers to treat their wives with more respect and not as a piece of property that they can dispose of when they tire of them. So, Jesus radically reformed Moses' divorce laws here, by compassionately providing women with more stability in their married lives. Same sex marriage did not exist in the day of our Lord Jesus Christ, and was not likely to in such a patriarchal culture, so it is a self-fulfilling prophecy that the Son of God would only talk about marriage between male and female (especially when scholars use His words out of context). Yet in many societies today, the Holy Spirit moves us to recognise that homosexuals have had their sexual orientation from birth. Let anyone accept this who can by allowing same sex couples to exchange marriage vows in church, just as heterosexual couples do.

Conservative Christians Worship the Word, instead of the Holy Spirit

Conservative Christians say that they cannot perform same sex marriage services because this is not part of the liturgy that the church has handed down to worshippers for generations. I say to the modern day Pharisees, that you are again worshipping the word, rather than the Holy Spirit. Besides, it is not as if the liturgy of the marriage service has always been the same. The Church of England, for instance, updated the 1662 *Book of Common Prayer* with *Common Worship* in 2000. In 2012, the US Episcopal Church provided a strong lead on the blessing of same sex unions by trialling a liturgy called "The Witnessing and Blessing of a Lifelong Covenant", which is the ideal basis for a same sex marriage service. Indeed, so close is it to a marriage service that the Episcopal Church has had to reiterate that it is merely a blessing, for fear of offending the Pharisees within the Anglican Communion.

Same Sex Marriage as a Moral Conscience Issue

The 2013 Church of England Pilling report offered the tantalising suggestion that churches could locally choose to hold services that 'marked' same sex unions (as even going as far as offering a 'blessing' for same sex unions would be going 'too far' for today's Pharisees). However, given that many countries in the Anglican Communion have a predominantly patriarchal culture (whose congregations regard the Bible as the literal word of God, and so they will take a long time to accept same sex marriages), I believe that there is no option but for Church of England parishes to initially hold same sex marriage services locally. I am sure of my arguments, and I am certain that same sex marriage will eventually be universally adopted by churches and states. However, in a bid to avoid disharmony within the Anglican Communion, I think that it is best for Parochial Church Councils to decide for themselves if they want to hold same sex marriage services, as this is very much a moral conscience issue. As I have already mentioned in this book, since it has taken the Church of England twenty years to decide on whether women priests can become bishops, then I expect that it will take equally long (if not longer) for the Church of England to adopt a national same sex marriage service. Yet the Church of England has to adopt same sex marriage in some form, otherwise the public will increasingly view its stance as being discriminatory to gay people, which will inevitably lead to even fewer people attending church. In the short term, I recognise that the Church of England adopting same sex marriage nationally could seriously affect the spread of the Gospel in patriarchal countries, until such time as the Holy Spirit removes the veil that hampers the sight of the Pharisees in these parts of the Anglican Communion. I must note here that the Church of England's House of Bishops rejected the Pilling report's recommendation that clergy be allowed to 'mark' same sex marriages. The House of Bishops also banned clergy from entering into civil same sex marriages, although they did allow clergy to enter into civil partnerships in the UK as long as they remain celibate, which, in the eyes of the general British public, is very discriminatory.

Churches that Welcome Same Sex Marriage

Obviously, same sex couples are free to marry in civil registry offices in many places throughout the world, but those of them that are Christian will want to marry in church, and it will be inequitable not to allow them to do so. However, hope is at hand, for there are Christian denominations in the UK where Pharisees are less numerous. The Unitarian Church has enthusiastically adopted same sex marriage, as have the Quakers. (On a side note, Liberal Judaism in the UK has also been a great proponent for same sex marriage.)

Reforming Churches do not Confine Sex to Procreation

Most Protestant denominations say that marital sexual pleasure is a gift from God, and allow contraception, in contrast to the Roman Catholic teaching that the main purpose of sex within marriage is procreation, which is why they ban contraception. So, the Protestant churches of the Reformation have already made take a huge stride towards same sex marriage by teaching that marital sexual pleasure is a gift from God that is not confined to procreation. If sex is not confined to procreation, then it follows that we should not deny this divine marital gift to same sex couples who are willing to commit to a lifelong union.

*

The Church of England's Commercialisation of Marriage

The Church of England's wedding website (yourchurchwedding.org) explicitly uses sex to sell their marriage services: "Marriage provides more and better sex" reads a banner that is on the website as I write. Although the fee that the Church of England charges for marriages is laid down in law (and according to yourchurchwedding.org is derived from the ancient custom of communities donating to their church), I am not sure that our Lord Jesus Christ would have approved of this commercialisation of marriage in church. For instance, when Jesus cleansed the Temple of all the merchants at Passover, He said "Stop making my Father's house a market-place!" (John 2:16, NRSVA). It is quite clear that the Church of England is making a big profit from the marriage service, as the basic set cost of £451 (in 2014) is far more than it actually costs for a church to hold such an event.

Love Your Neighbour as Yourself

In case any Christians are still confused about which of the laws of Moses they should follow, this is what our Lord Jesus Christ had to say about them when the Pharisees challenged Him (Matthew 22:34-40):

> When the Pharisees heard that he had silenced the Sadducees, they gathered together, and one of them, a lawyer, asked him a question to test him. 'Teacher, which commandment in the law is the greatest?' He said to him, '"You shall love the Lord your God with all your heart, and with all your soul, and with all your mind." This is the greatest and first commandment. And a second is like it: "You shall love your neighbour as yourself." On these two commandments hang all the law and the prophets.' (NRSVA)

These are the two commandments that Christians should follow in their everyday lives, rather than harking back to Moses' laws. Indeed, this was a very good answer from Jesus to silence the Pharisees, as "You shall love your neighbour as yourself" was originally an injunction from the Lord to the Israelites, which Moses transcribed (Leviticus 19:18). Although Jesus said that He did not come to abolish the law (the Ten Commandments, rather than the laws of Moses), but to fulfil it (Matthew 5:17-18), He did very much refine it, just as He reversed Adam and Eve's punitive expulsion from the paradise of Eden by offering the penitent eternal salvation after He had died on the cross for our sins. The Archbishop of Canterbury has said that one of the main reasons why the Church of England has not changed its doctrine on homosexuality is due to 'neighbour love'; meaning that he, as the head of the Anglican Communion, must respect and listen to the views of overseas conservative Anglican Christians while the Church deliberates at length upon the issue of homosexuality. However, the main thrust of my argument is that conservative Christians' denigration of gay people is wholly incompatible with the concept of neighbour love, and so the complete acceptance of gay people should take priority over acceding to the views of conservative Christians.

Conservative Christians are Contrary to the Sermon on the Mount When They Condemn Homosexuality

Our Lord Jesus Christ stated in his Beatitudes, "Blessed are you when people revile you and persecute you and utter all kinds of evil against you falsely on my account" (Matthew 5:11, NRSVA). He was talking about how His disciples would inevitably be persecuted for spreading the Gospel. However, I believe this beatitude also holds true when conservative Christians falsely condemn homosexuality in the name of our Lord Jesus Christ, for it is entirely contrary to the spirit of the Sermon on the Mount for conservative Christians to do this. Today's Pharisees must question themselves whether, by denying same sex marriage, they are treating their gay neighbours as equals (as James the Just commanded that they should). I have no doubt that today's Pharisees will be greatly angered when Christian churches adopt same sex marriage, and that they will argue that this it has no place within the traditional rituals of the church. However, the only sacrament that our Lord Jesus Christ directly passed down to us was Holy Communion, and not these other rituals.

We Must Forgive Those That Condemn Homosexuality by Joining Them in Communion

I hope and pray that today's Pharisees will eventually acknowledge their sin of refusing to accept our prodigal sons and daughters as they are, and that they will finally welcome gay people, and feast with them in Holy Communion in our Father's House, as our Lord Jesus Christ instructed them to do in The Parable of the Lost Son and the Self-righteous Son. Although it pains me when a Pharisee speaks out against homosexuality, due to their veiled view of scripture, I will still happily enter into communion with them, for I understand why they do it and I forgive them. Do not forget that James the Just also wrote the following with regards to neighbour love (James 4:11-12):

> Do not speak evil against one another, brothers and sisters. Whoever speaks evil against another or judges another, speaks evil against the law and judges the law; but if you judge the law, you are not a doer of the law but a judge. There is one lawgiver and judge who is able to save and to destroy. So who, then, are you to judge your neighbour?

Mercy Triumphs over Judgement

As James the Just teaches us, I appeal to conservative Christians to no longer speak out against your homosexual neighbours, especially as James also wrote:

> So speak and so act as those who are to be judged by the law of liberty. For judgement will be without mercy to anyone who has shown no mercy; mercy triumphs over judgement. (James 2:12-13)

In time, I hope to win over all the Pharisees with my arguments, and that we can all say *amen* on this debate; however, I must admit that there will always be Pharisees with hard hearts that I will never persuade. My arguments will anger these Pharisees; yet I hope that they will not divorce themselves from the Anglican Communion if the Holy Spirit does lead the Church of England and other denominations to accept same sex marriage, and to change its doctrine on homosexuality. Indeed, via the parable discussed in this chapter, Jesus made it quite clear that such self-righteous sons should not divorce themselves from their church.

*

Mercy, not Sacrifice

Mine is not the only book that has sought to redefine the way that Christianity deals with homosexuality. Matthew Vines' book *God and the Gay Christian* has caused a bigger stir than this volume so far, which is probably due to Vines being (as I mentioned earlier) a much more eloquent speaker than I am. What I have found interesting is that when journals have published negative reviews of *God and the Gay Christian*, they have sometimes done so by selecting a gay Christian that has adopted celibacy to review the book. For instance, Sam Alberry's review of *God and the Gay Christian* for *The Gospel Coalition* criticised Vines' book as not being "kind enough" by offering false hope to gay Christians. Likewise, Christopher Yuan's review in *Christianity Today* chimes very well with the themes of my final chapter:

> Too often, we are more like the older, self-righteous brother of the prodigal son, and our hearts are hardened toward the lost. This is truth at the expense of grace. But the approach that Vines suggests—grace at the expense of truth—also misses the mark. It overlooks the theology of suffering and gives us Christ without the Cross. Jesus, who personifies love, came full of grace and full of truth (John 1:14). Might this be how we live as well.

Both Yuan and Alberry mention the struggles that they have had in coming to terms with their sexual orientation, which they believe flies in the face of scripture:

> This is not to say that the church has been perfect on this issue. Nor is it to say that life as a Christian with same-sex attraction is easy. There can be deep pains: battling with desires we wish we did not have, times of isolation and loneliness, and the absence of romantic companionship. (Alberry)

> We have failed to provide gospel-centered support for same-sex attracted Christians. As a 43-year-old single man *who did not choose singleness*, I know firsthand the challenges of obedience. (Yuan)

However, I say to Alberry, Yuan, and every other gay Christian that has chosen celibacy because they think homosexuality is a sin that they should think again. As Jesus himself told the Pharisees, "I desire mercy, not sacrifice" (Matthew 9:13, NRSVA). By all means, stay celibate if you think that this will bring you closer to God, but do not do so because you think homosexuality is a sin, for such a sacrifice is pointless. Do not torture yourself, for by so doing, you are disobeying Christ's synthesis of the law: "You shall love your neighbour as *yourself*." If you do not truly love yourself, and the life that the Lord has given you, then how can you truly love your neighbour without resentment? You have only one life, so do not torment yourself.

Why Do We Criticise and Judge Each Other?

Then again, I am mindful that Paul, like James, told us that we should not criticise other Christians that have different beliefs from us (Romans 14:1-4):

> Welcome those who are weak in faith, but not for the purpose of quarrelling over opinions. Some believe in eating anything, while the weak eat only vegetables. Those who eat must not despise those who abstain, and those who abstain must not pass judgement on those who eat; for God has welcomed them. Who are you to pass judgement on servants of another? It is before their own lord that they stand or fall. (NRSVA)

Indeed, this brings to mind Pope Francis's recent comment on gay people: "If a person seeks God and has goodwill, then who am I to judge?" What appears to be an off-the-cuff remark by the pontiff has a sound scriptural basis, derived from Paul and James's commandments that we should not judge other Christians.

Church Law Causes (Rather Than Settles) Disputes

What is it that brings liberals and conservatives to blows over issues such as homosexuality? What is it that increases the heat of such arguments? Why do we criticise each other? We do so because many of our churches have 'laws' on teachings. So to win the debate means that we have to have heated internecine battles, as changing the 'law' means that there will always be a losing side, which will be bitter at the prospect of defeat. For instance, as I was doing the final edit of this book, Pope Francis was defeated in his bid for the Catholic Church to have a more welcoming dialogue with gay and divorced people. Just like the Church of England synod, this Roman Catholic Family Synod had to have a two thirds majority to pass new motions into law, instead of just a simple majority, which means that it is next to impossible to pass new liberal church laws on issues such as homosexuality in bodies where there is a majority of conservative voices. I must commend Pope Francis on his more positive stance on homosexuality when compared to his predecessors; although I must point out that there was never any chance that the Catholic Church would adopt same sex marriage at this Family Synod.

To Increase Diversity, We Must Abolish Church Laws That Restrict Teaching Derived from Scripture

Rather than trying to change these church laws so that the liberal view of homosexuality predominates instead of the conservative one, I argue that we must get rid of such 'laws' on Church teaching, as they cause nothing but dispute. Let those who believe that same sex marriage is permissible under the new covenant go ahead with it, while those who believe in only heterosexual marriage should be free to follow their principles, as they too consider that they are justified in scripture. Both sides can still debate the issue, but in a less cut-throat atmosphere, which will still allow them to break bread together afterwards. In writing this, I am mindful of Pope Francis' warning to liberal members of the 2014 Catholic Family Synod that they should avoid their usual temptation to resort to the "deceptive mercy [that] binds the wounds without first curing them and treating them; that treats the symptoms and not the causes and the roots." Indeed, the first edition of this book had more a "put up and shut up" tone towards conservative Christians, which would have merely put their backs up and made them more defensive, instead of accommodating my new arguments.

The Return of the Broad Church Perspective

It was necessary in the early days of the Church to have judgements (such as James the Just's ruling at the Council of Jerusalem in 50 AD) that settled disputes and provided clarity. However, now that the Christian Church is the world's largest religion two thousand years later, and its future is therefore secure, Christianity is in the enviable position of being able to be honest and open that it does not know all the answers, and that its members, although they share the same faith, can hold some quite contrasting beliefs. At its zenith in the 19th Century, the Church of England regarded itself as a "Broad Church", composed of liberal and conservative individuals (and those in between), and this is a more realistic representation of all churches today. Instead of churches proclaiming that "We teach this, that and the other", they should instead declare that "Some of us believe this, while others believe that." The truth is that we are still learning about this wonderful world that God has created for us, and we still do not know all the whole truth. As Paul wrote in 2 Corinthians 3:7-8, this is now the "Ministry of the Spirit", not "the Ministry of Death, chiselled in letters on stone tablets".

This is a Living, Breathing Church

This is a living, breathing Church, capable of change and evolution, not a monolithic, static Church redolent of rigor mortis. As Paul also writes, the Lord our God will pass final judgement on us. I solemnly believe that homosexuality is not a sin, and that it would be merciful for us to finally recognise our LGBT brothers and sisters for who they are, and that we should no longer treat them differently from heterosexuals, as James the Just commands. If am wrong, then the Lord will judge me for this. Similarly, if conservative Christians are wrong in their belief that homosexuality is a sin; the Lord will judge them for this also.

The Abolition of Inequitable Church Laws

Since I believe that I have provided a good scriptural case for LGBT people to be treated equally in the issue of marriage and all rituals of the Church, I now ask that churches throughout the world to strike out any church law that treats LGBT people any differently than heterosexuals, as these are the laws of the "ministry of death". For instance, I ask that churches not only perform marriage ceremonies for same sex couples, but also that they remove restrictions such as the Church of England's requirement that gay clergy remain celibate, and the ban against gay clergy marrying same sex partners. In return, conservative Christians will still be free to preach their own belief that homosexuality is a sin, and to only perform heterosexual marriages.

There are Many Paths to Salvation

In His wisdom, our Lord Jesus Christ foresaw that there will always be quarrels between the liberals and conservatives of the Church. However, as Jesus taught us in the Parable of the Lost Son and the Self-righteous Son, we can have consolation that our Heavenly Father unquestionably loves both the liberals and the conservatives of his flock, despite the tendency of both of us to stray. It would seem that there is not one path that leads us to salvation (or just the two paths of the liberals and conservatives); for we each have our own path to God.

###

Kevin Mahoney is the author of the novel *A Fame of Two Halves*, *The Cuban Missile Crisis - American Decision Making During October 1962*, *Steven Moffat's Doctor Who 2010*, *Steven Moffat's Doctor Who 2011*, and *Steven Moffat's Doctor Who 2012-2013*.

Punked Books are also the publishers of:

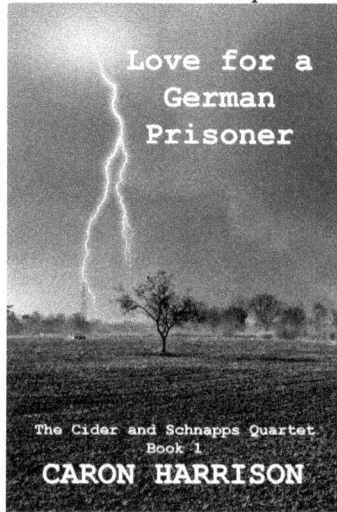

A powerful story of love and forgiveness
Love for a German Prisoner by Caron Harrison

Who is truly free?
Katherine Carter believes she is. With all her life spent on her father's Herefordshire farm, her future seems mapped out - until she meets Karl. Karl Driesler has little freedom. His future is bleak. Still a prisoner of war eighteen months after Germany's surrender, he suffers nightmares, and his fiancée has just married another man.
Robert Murdoch, the village doctor's son, also suffers nightmares. A former prisoner of the Japanese, he finds freedom unexpectedly hard to cope with - until he meets Karl.
These three find their growing bonds of friendship and love tested to the full as Karl's past catches up with him. Denied the freedom to love, Karl's world is shattered, while Katherine's is thrown into turmoil.

This is Caron Harrison's debut novel, originally published in 1997 under the title of *Shades of Grey*, and the first volume in *The Cider and Schnapps Quartet*.

www.ingramcontent.com/pod-product-compliance
Lightning Source LLC
Chambersburg PA
CBHW071845020426
42331CB00007B/1867